THE TECHNOLOGIZED INVESTOR

THE TECHNOLOGIZED INVESTOR

Innovation through Reorientation

Ashby H.B. Monk and Dane Rook

STANFORD BUSINESS BOOKS

An Imprint of Stanford University Press • Stanford, California

Stanford University Press

Stanford, California

Special discounts for bulk quantities of Stanford Business Books are available to corporations, professional associations, and other organizations. For details and discount information, contact the special sales department of Stanford University Press. Tel: (650) 725-0820, Fax: (650) 725-3457

Printed in the United States of America on acid-free, archival-quality paper

Library of Congress Cataloging-in-Publication Data

Names: Monk, Ashby H. B. (Ashby Henry Benning), 1976- author. | Rook, Dane, 1986- author.

Title: The technologized investor : innovation through reorientation / Ashby H. B. Monk and Dane Rook.

Description: Stanford, California : Stanford Business Books, an imprint of Stanford University Press, 2020. | Includes bibliographical references and index. |

Identifiers: LCCN 2019037479 (print) | LCCN 2019037480 (ebook) | ISBN 9781503608696 (cloth) | ISBN 9781503612099 (epub)

Subjects: LCSH: Investments--Technological innovations. | Institutional investments--Technological innovations.

Classification: LCC HG4515.5 .M655 2020 (print) | LCC HG4515.5 (ebook) | DDC 332.6--dc23

LC record available at https://lccn.loc.gov/2019037479

LC ebook record available at https://lccn.loc.gov/2019037480

Cover design: Tandem Creative

Typeset by Newgen in Minion Pro and 11/15 point

CONTENTS

ACKNOWLEDGMENTS

This project wouldn't have gone anywhere without the generosity, patience, and good humor of a very large number of practitioners and academic colleagues—of whom there are too many to thank in the space here. Nonetheless, our sincerest gratitude goes to all who have helped on this book and the work that has preceded it. There are, however, some individuals who have been especially involved in our research and who deserve our direct recognition: Peter Curtis, Ray Levitt, Joe Lonsdale, Daniel Nadler, Kanishk Parashar, Marcel Prins, David Sara, and Rajiv Sharma. We'd also like to thank our families for putting up with us during the long course of this project—and for putting up with us in general. Finally, we reserve our most heartfelt thanks for our mentor, Gordon L. Clark. This book is dedicated to all of the invaluable lessons he's taught us over the years, and we wish him all the best in his much-deserved retirement (although we wager that he'll still find ways to actively keep helping the Investor world!).

INTRODUCTION

A Need for Heroes

There seems to be something fundamental in human nature that makes us love superheroes. We've been imagining, idolizing, and celebrating them for millennia. The ancient Greeks revered Perseus, Achilles, and Heracles.[1] Ancient Sumerians exalted the heroism of Enkidu. Cú Chulainn is lionized in Celtic tradition. Maori lore venerates Maui. Norse mythology features far too many super-beings to mention. And Hollywood mints multiple blockbuster movies every year that feed our fascination with superheroes and their extraordinary powers.

But it's more than superpowers that gives superheroes their enduring, widespread allure. Superheroes are inspiring because they fix major problems that no one else can, which frequently entails saving the world. In most instances, superheroes possess their superpowers *before* facing these challenges. Some recently popular superheroes, however, break this pattern. They actively build special powers *in response* to the crises they tackle. And they use advanced technology to do so (think Iron Man and Batman). They transform from being mere mortals into superhumans by *technologizing*.

The world currently needs more real-life versions of these technologized superheroes to solve some of its otherwise intractable problems.

An expanding wealth gap between the rich and poor threatens socio-economic disruption. A shortage of modernized, reliable infrastructure depresses the quality of life for billions of people worldwide, even in many first-world countries. Climate change and environmental degradation—fueled by unsustainable production, transportation, and disposal practices—threaten the viability of many (human and nonhuman) communities in both the developed and developing world. And demographic shifts are making it increasingly hard for governments to help citizens who are elderly, unhealthy, or underprivileged.

Despite their diverse causes, each of these existential threats to humankind's health and happiness could be mitigated by the availability and responsible deployment of more long-term funding. However, with banks constrained by new regulations and governments tightening budgets, the remaining organizations that could be delivering the vast majority of that funding—the world's long-term asset owners, for example, public pension funds, sovereign wealth funds, endowments, and foundations—are deprived of the resources they need to do so. This may come as a surprise, as one might naturally question: "Don't these organizations together manage around $100 trillion in investable capital? Surely, that's sufficient to resolve the aforementioned problems and still have plenty of dough leftover!"[2]

Sadly, that's not so. And, problematically, the organizations appointed to invest that capital aren't allowed to tap enough of it to grow it, or their organizations, to the extent needed to solve these problems. That is, long-term asset owners (also called institutional investors, and hereafter, "Investors") aren't presently set up such that their investment and operating activities properly align with their long-term time horizons—even though some of the planet's gravest challenges would be closer to being solved if they were!

Instead, most Investors are held captive by their own *context*. Investors are disadvantaged by the exploitative ecosystem that has cropped up around them and is riddled with intermediaries who charge extortionate fees, distort risks, and chronically deliver flimsy results. Investors are also disadvantaged by their own governance structures, which are often imposed on them by sponsoring entities that are highly politi-

cized (e.g., unions, local governments) but not necessarily fluent in finance. And Investors are disadvantaged by being starved of the resources to innovate and adapt to a world that's ever changing in all
domains—not just in finance. Shockingly, these disadvantages persist
despite the fact that Investors are the very anchor of our capitalist
system.

To overcome these disadvantages, Investors need to become technological marvels. They need superhero-like technology that can help
them understand their liabilities, their assets, their people, and their
progress toward success. This book is a "flight manual" for Investors
interested in becoming technologically empowered superheroes capable of delivering high risk-adjusted returns while also solving major
global problems.[3] A few intrepid Investors—in Canada, the Nether-
lands, Australia, and elsewhere—have already begun this transformation. Others are only pondering their metamorphosis or have yet to
even realize the possibility. Yet we believe they *all* can technologize.

Our central thesis is that all Investors can utterly transform their
capability sets by adopting advanced technology and making it integral
to how they manage innovation, data, and knowledge. But such superpowers can't be gained by simply 'bolting on' advanced technology to
their existing resources and processes. Instead, Investors must reorient
themselves around new technologies. Reorientation won't necessarily
be easy. It'll require changing mindsets, priorities, and cultures. Nonetheless, Investors must succeed in making this transition: failure is far
too costly, and no one else will be coming to the rescue. To succeed,
however, Investors must bypass their weaknesses.

All superheroes have weaknesses. Some are mundane (exposed
heels, haircuts, asbestos, and low batteries). Others are exotic (kryptonite, adamantium, electromagnetic pulses, and Muramasa Blades).
We've already mentioned how present context is a weakness for most
Investors. Yet context-generated disadvantages really only feed Investors' chief weakness: the lure of short-termism. Short-termism devas-
tates Investors by trapping them in an unwinnable game that blocks
them from innovating, and therefore impedes their long-term success.[4]
Focusing on short horizons also prevents them from using their greatest

strength: the fact that they can adopt long-term views and ownership positions in assets in ways that no other financial entities can.

But Investors have other native advantages beyond just long horizons. Some Investors have an edge due to geography (e.g., they may be located near entrepreneurial hubs and so have ready access to path-breaking start-ups).[5] Others may be affiliated with universities or similar research institutions that afford them expert insight into niche opportunities. Still others may have special relationships with host governments that allow them an inside track on investing in assets like infrastructure or energy. This text is a playbook to help Investors deploy advanced technologies that leverage their unique advantages—not only to overcome their disadvantages, but also to turn them into strengths (and, dare we hope, superpowers).

Can Investors actually achieve these objectives? Are these declarations just miscalibrated optimism by a pair of social scientists who have toiled too long in academia and are out of touch with the realities of institutional investing? We answer a humble "No" to the second question and an exuberant "Yes!" to the first. It's true we're academic researchers. Still, many of our university colleagues would consider us as much practitioners as academicians (and possibly even more of the former). We spend most of our waking hours meeting with, calling, and working alongside Investors—not cloistered in ivory towers and libraries. Our viewpoint is informed by thousands of hours spent in the field, conversing with hundreds of Investors from across the globe about all aspects of their operations. All of that close dialogue and interaction has been further informed by our involvement with Investors on their innovation projects. Additionally, we've even taken the leap into building companies in the space, as both of us have started or worked at multiple "invest-tech" outfits that target the nexus of long-term investing and advanced technology. Together, these experiences fully convince us that successful technological reorientation is attainable for Investors. We wholeheartedly believe technologized Investors can save capitalism and humankind by overcoming their pervasive governance constraints, cultural limitations, geographic isolation, fear of innovation, and all the other challenges the Investor community faces. This book presents our rationale and the evidence we've found for having that faith.

Leapfrogging: From Intelligent to Technologized

By now, some readers undoubtedly will think we're crazy in asserting that technology could lead Investors to a new state of mastery over their operations and portfolios. Technology is a weak point for most Investors, right? So why are these guys suggesting Investors use *advanced* technology to fix their problems, especially when they're struggling to use what they've got now? Before you accuse us of quackery, hear us out: what we propose isn't more of the same. In fact, the specific possibilities that we're describing depart from the status quo in three key ways. We're saying Investors can utilize advanced tech to

- cultivate and leverage their native advantages;
- more tightly align their present resources and long-term goals, by ultimately amplifying those resources; and
- foster deeper innovation.

Each of these marks a pivotal departure from technology's current role in Investors' organizations, but the last is probably the most essential. Currently, most Investors struggle to innovate and are held back from innovating by inadequate technology. Technology should stoke innovation, not stymie it![6] The view of technologizing we present in this book doesn't involve some transplant, whereby existing, underperforming tech gets swapped out for breakthrough technology. No, our version of technologizing is more symbiotic and focused on empowering organizations to make them excel at innovating. Yes, building an innovative pension fund may seem quixotic—or even oxymoronic. But the reality is that there's a dire need to inject innovation into a community of organizations that has been far too conservative for far too long.

As we show in the following chapters, infusions of advanced tech into the organization must be done in ways that integrate with other organizational processes and resources, such as culture, governance, strategy, risk management, and—*especially*—innovation. To us, a one-two punch of advanced technology and deeper innovation is a kind of judo move that will help Investors *leapfrog* in two ways. First, it will let them skip from being tech laggards in the financial community to tech leaders—bypassing along the way all of the middling funds and firms stuck between their legacy systems and cutting-edge solutions. Second, it will let them unshackle themselves from exploitative intermediaries and finally innovate for themselves, as opposed to outsourcing technology and innovation to misaligned outsiders.

Investors have a lengthy history of paying third parties, such as external asset managers, to innovate and deploy new technologies on their behalves. On its surface, this outsourcing may seem sensible for organizations like Investors that are hamstrung by diminutive operating budgets. Over the long term, however, it's a recipe for debilitating dependence. When Investors pay other parties for these pursuits, they subsidize those parties' superior innovation and technological capabilities. In doing so, Investors widen the rift between those capabilities and their own—all without ensuring that the third-party capabilities they're subsidizing actually serve Investors' own best interests!

Imagine what would be possible if fees that Investors pay for outsourcing these capabilities were diverted to build up their own technology and innovation systems. Just think: if, collectively, Investors spent a mere 10 basis points of their total assets under management on technology and innovation, then they'd surpass the annual technology and innovation budgets for Apple, Amazon, Facebook, Google, Microsoft, and IBM . . . COMBINED.[7]

Of course, spending doesn't immediately translate to innovation: those six companies are all engineered around technological innovation. It's their raison d'être, whereas technology and innovation are just a means to an end (of high risk-adjusted returns in the long run) for Investors. Nevertheless, technology and innovation need capital to flourish and, right now, Investors are woefully underspending on both. Investors typically spend just 1 or 2 basis points (0.01–0.02%) of the total assets in their care on technology, data, research, innovation, and related efforts. Contrast that with the 50 or more (sometimes way more) basis points routinely spent on fees to external asset managers. Many Investors tolerate this differential because they feel those managers are "superior" at using technology and innovating. But is it sane to think that external managers are doing so 20, 50, or even 100 times better than Investors could do themselves? We doubt it. We think the money that's been subsidizing other parties' technology (and mediocre results) could be used more intelligently.

Our book's title pays homage to Benjamin Graham's masterpiece, *The Intelligent Investor.* That book's release was a watershed in the history of finance. Before it, investing was largely equated with speculation and gambling—in other words, trying to game the market over the short haul. Graham instead articulated how sustained performance could be achieved from the starting point of understanding an asset, by studying its fundamental value drivers, and then judiciously buying that asset when its inferred value exceeds its price. The approach advocated by Graham came to be known as *value investing,* and his contribution to it wasn't solely theoretical: wise ol' Benjie was reported to have generated an average annual return of 20 percent over several decades of stock market investing. Likewise, his most famous protégé (the quintessential long-term investor), Warren Buffett, has followed Graham's core approach to reliably deliver similar returns over an even longer horizon.[8]

Despite their reasonability and demonstrable success, the chief tenets of *The Intelligent Investor* have taken backstage to those of so-called modern finance, which attempts to replace understanding with simplistic quantification (e.g., via formulaic diversification, a blind faith in efficient markets, and vehement disbelief in durable advantages). Oddly, this upstaging seems to have less to do with performance and more to do with marketability. It's easier to sell financial "products" in the modern paradigm than the value-based paradigm. Unfortunately, Investors often get caught up in this sleight of hand. In many ways, *The Technologized Investor* is a revisiting of the eminently sensible ideas on long-term investing that were first posited in *The Intelligent Investor.* Pointedly, our objective here isn't to supplant those ideas: it's to augment them. In short, we think Investors can become better value investors with the right selection and deployment of advanced technology.

Reading the Flight Manual

An aircraft's flight manual is a document that contains the information needed to *safely* operate it. Compared with the complexity of the aircraft itself, the flight manual is a fairly succinct document that's meant for easy reference (from the operator's perspective). It describes in detail how, from a functional viewpoint, various parts of the aircraft work, their limitations, and what corrective action to take when things aren't going right. While it's best to read the flight manual cover-to-cover, one can also use it by jumping straight to relevant topics of interest (or urgent need), without having looked at the preceding material.[9]

We've labored to ensure this book is a flight manual for technologizing Investors. It's not as exhaustive as a longer, more prescriptive treatment (such as a pilot's operating handbook) might be. Rather, its job is to convey the needed background and then quickly get to the practical points. Nor is it like a textbook on aerospace engineering or the mathematics of turbulence: instead, it's a user-centric guide for those *flying* the craft. It doesn't specify exactly what to do in every situation; but it does give an accessible rundown of how to diagnose problems, where to look for solutions, and what to check when analyzing whether a candidate solution might work for the issues at hand.

That said, given the complexity of the topics this manual must cover, it necessarily spans a large amount of conceptual territory. Different readers will almost surely find some parts of this book more valuable than others, as their specific interests or their organizations' contexts dictate. Nevertheless, there's a small raft of ideas that we think any reader should absorb, regardless of her reason for cracking open this book (whether in its entirety or only for a particular topic):

- The chief way in which technology can help Investors reach their long-term goals is through allowing them to build and extend competitive advantages in *accessing* and *understanding* specific types of opportunities and risks, both outside and inside their own organizations.

- Data, information, and knowledge are separate resources that require their own management and governance processes. They can, however, be converted into one another—especially with the help of advanced technologies.

- The importance of unconventional data for decision making is on the rise for Investors. This *alternative data* can come from many sources and have many uses, but the most valuable of these are usually within an Investor's internal operations. Indeed, efficiency enhancements to their own operations are some of the most durably valuable changes an Investor can make with technology, because these operational changes typically aren't assailable by outside parties.

- Finding aligned technology partners—whether start-ups, peers, or other entities—can be a core part of an Investor's long-term success in technologizing and deepening its capacity for innovation.

- Innovation—whether with or without technology—is very much an outcome of consistent processes and dedicated resources. It requires a culture that is able to embrace learning and uncertainty, to accept controlled failure, and to act scientifically in a continual effort to improve.

These ideas are woven throughout the book: each appears to some degree and in some form within practically every chapter.

To enable readers to have a crisper picture of what's in this flight manual (beyond just what's listed in the Table of Contents), here's a brief sketch of each chapter.

Chapter 1: History of Investment Technology
We lead a whirlwind, curated tour of investment technology's six-millennium history—from clay tablets on up to digital ones. We tease out three dimensions of progress that have characterized advances in

invest-tech across time: data latency, inferential depth, and resource efficiency. We discuss patterns in how these dimensions are interrelated, and why they're important for technologizing Investors. We also look at how the tyrannous reign of spreadsheets is a posterchild for what's presently amiss with investment technology.

Chapter 2: Technology Problems in Institutional Investing
We conduct a deep-dive appraisal of the state of technology in institutional investing and dissect how it's holding Investors back from attaining their goals. We discuss ten "entangling" problems that our research indicates are to blame, including focusing on the wrong scales for tech projects, deprioritizing innovation, having isolated perspectives about technology, failing to cooperate with peers on tech, and more. We also explain why some "scapegoats" that get blamed for Investors' tech troubles are mostly just hollow excuses (these include outsourcing, cost, and being "close followers").

Chapter 3: Technology Trends and Tools
We provide an overview of current trends in cutting-edge technology that are relevant for technologizing Investors, with special attention to two: openness and simplicity. We cover four key classes of tools that can serve as the foundations of technologized Investors' tech superpowers: artificial intelligence, alternative data, collaboration tools, and productivity utilities. We discuss the balance that must be struck between understanding and efficiently deploying these tools. In the appendix, we give flyovers of deep-learning and blockchain fundamentals.

Chapter 4: Frameworks for Technology Analysis
We supply rubrics to help Investors analyze the suitability of specific technologies for their organizations. We begin by introducing a tool set to compare a candidate technology's impacts on the organization's opportunity set and resource budget. We then provide several tools for analyzing how a technology may affect, and create value from, an organization's data, information, and knowledge resources. We conclude

with commentary about the role of cost-benefit analysis in assessing technology's fitness within the organization.

Chapter 5: Template for a Technologized Investor
We present thirteen features that our research indicates any successfully technologized Investor should exhibit. Some of these can be quickly attainable, whereas others may take time to grow. To further understanding, we split these features into two groups: *Core Attributes* needed to sustain tech skills in the long run; and *Sources of Advantage* that'll more immediately help Investors brandish tech superpowers.

Chapter 6: Data Empowerment
We begin our foray into the data-related tech superpowers Investors can build. We distill our empirical findings on causes of Investors' current discontentment with their existing data systems. We discuss several ways in which Investors could beneficially *rethink* data by: merging data-governance and data-management protocols; casting data as a collective process; focusing on retaining and augmenting more context around data sets; prioritizing data on unlisted, private assets; and nixing the binary treatment of data systems (i.e., seeing things through a federated vs. centralized lens). We propose enhancements to the "people side" of Investors' data systems, including a need for global-local comprehension and coordinated entrepreneurship around organizational data.

Chapter 7: Equipping Data Empowerment
We inspect a suite of tech platforms and tools to enable data empowerment for Investors. We study tools for transforming data, enhancing it, and extracting crucial insights from it, including metadata, inference algorithms, data-workflow pipelines, tools for breaking the tyranny of spreadsheets, and visualization utilities. We cover problems that Investors have with existing database architectures and tour some advanced solutions that could support data-empowerment programs well into the future.

Chapter 8: Reframing Risk Management
We explain some terminal difficulties with risk-management tools from modern finance and say some heretical things about conventional approaches to portfolio diversification—for example, it's actually an expensive (not free) lunch for long-term Investors and a dangerous starting point for portfolio construction and risk management. We introduce a replacement approach to managing risk that's better geared toward long-term Investors, especially technologizing ones. We explore how three categories of technology—alternative data, knowledge-management tools, and smart contracts—can put this new approach into action.

Chapter 9: Technologized Risk Exposure
We delve into technology that can help Investors more dexterously manage their exposures to risk. We investigate the importance of *exposure purity* and how technology can assist in cultivating and maintaining it. We explore advanced technologies that can assist Investors in pursuing exposure purity via asset allocation, benchmarking, achieving flexible access to investment opportunities, and cooperativity.

Chapter 10: Space to Innovate
We investigate best practices and Investors' direct experiences with making innovation and technology both more complementary and programmatic. We study lessons learned by some pioneering Investors in their attempts at infusing more innovative mindsets, processes, and forcing mechanisms into their organizations. We look into the essential contributions made by the "softer side" of innovation, in terms of the importance of a culture of learning, ways to preserve enough of the right types of resources to fuel innovation for the long term, and innovation partnerships.

Chapter 11: Spinning Up R3D Teams
We give an in-depth case study of a revolutionary approach to programmatic innovation: the creation of an in-house task force to drive technological innovativeness. We describe four Investors' activities in

transitioning to this approach, in terms of design choices they made and frameworks they used to guide their thinking. We discuss implications of this achievement for other Investors—namely, as an illustration of what game-changing possibilities lie ahead.

Chapter 12: Getting Started
We conclude with a pep talk for readers on how their organizations can take the very first steps on the road to technologizing—and become true superheroes in so doing. We offer detailed pointers on the initial moves to make when putting this book's lessons into practice. We give one last rallying cry on how essential it is for Investors to collaborate with start-ups, as well as each other, in technologizing and innovating—in order to deliver an overall brighter future for us all.

Finding Our Cyborg Muse

The two authors of this book each began exploring these ideas over a decade ago—well before we began working together directly. We both have long sought ways to help Investors improve their performance potentials, by either altering their positions in the financial ecosystem or changing aspects of their own organizations. Yet we both encountered repeated frustration in our searches to improve governance, culture, risk management, and arrangements with intermediaries: each of these seemingly viable avenues for Investors to empower themselves proved to be ploddingly slow and vexingly difficult to change. In 2015, we came to the joint realization that technology might be an area where more traction would be possible; we wondered if technology could be the crack in the door to empowering Investors that we'd been seeking. We've been trying to test the limits of that possibility ever since (and we plan to keep on doing so!).

This book isn't your typical academic text. First, it's (as economic geographers would be inclined to say) *synoptic*. It captures the experiences and learnings conveyed to us by the Investors with whom we've had the immense privilege of working closely. But it also encapsulates our own hard-won insights from having worked among Investors, start-ups, venture capitalists, consultants, bankers, and more than our fair share of brilliant academics. And across those many interactions, we noticed a shocking lack of helpful, empirically grounded literature to aid Investors in their attempts to make better use of technology. This book was born out of our desire to close that void.

Second, we've done what we can to make our treatment both practical and approachable. A rule we set for ourselves from this project's start was that it needed to lead to actionable findings. No highfalutin theory or overwrought, hypertechnical analysis—just grounded recommendations informed by methodical observations (along with sporadic superhero references).[10]

There's one target we've observed since our project formally began that's been a continual source of inspiration, and amazement, to us. Like millions of others, we've been enthralled by the achievements of the AlphaGo program created by Google DeepMind.[11] We watched in astonishment as DeepMind's algorithmic creation beat the world's human champions at a game that's fiendishly more complex than chess: go. AlphaGo wasn't winning against human opponents by outpowering them with brute-force computation. It was using *genuine creativity* to come up with strategies that no person had previously conceived— or possibly ever could. We were wowed by its storied thirty-seventh move in its second game against Lee Sedol in 2016, its handy defeat of the world champ, Ke Jie, in 2017, and its eventual achievement of relearning go from scratch without witnessing any human moves (or outside coaching) whatsoever.[12] What struck us most profoundly, however, was a less publicized contribution: how greatly AlphaGo could improve human performance by working *alongside* people rather than against them.

During the same tournament in which AlphaGo defeated Ke Jie, a pairs session was held, where human players teamed with AlphaGo against other human players. AlphaGo and its human partner would alternate in playing moves against their noncyborg opponent.[13] Thore Graepel, who was part of the AlphaGo development team (and had a 1-dan rating at the time) said the following after playing a rehearsal pairs game as AlphaGo's partner: "By observing AlphaGo's moves, it

somehow raises your game. . . . I was able to contribute." Graepel estimates that his own standard of play—in terms of the moves he personally selected—was raised by 3 or 4 dan levels as a result of the scenarios
in which AlphaGo's moves put him. This type of cyborg mutualism—
with machines and technology empowering people to be far better than
they otherwise could—is what excites us most about the possibility of
technologized Investors. It's what gives us the most faith in the future.

CHAPTER 1   HISTORY OF INVESTMENT TECHNOLOGY

Why History Matters: Three-Dimensional Evolution

A crucial finding from our research is that most Investors are failing to use advanced technologies. Yet equally important is our finding that many Investors are also struggling to effectively use and manage the technology they already have. There's an evident need for change. But some context is required to pinpoint what *kinds* of change are necessary, and how to better help them succeed. Namely, it's vital to appreciate an organization's trajectory. And doing that involves grasping its past to understand the history of its operating environment.[1]

We therefore present a history that's pertinent to all Investors: the history of investment technology ("invest-tech") in general.[2] Doing so gives a richer explanation for why things are the way they are, and yields insights into where they're headed. Detouring into invest-tech's history is also worthwhile because it exposes deeper patterns in how technology at large evolves over time (and invest-tech along with it). Appreciating and planning around these patterns can help Investors build technology strategies that'll succeed over long horizons, since these patterns identify the technological advantages that are best positioned to persist, and even deepen, well into the future.[3] Our work suggests that the dominant patterns in invest-tech's evolution are three-dimensional. Practically every major advance in invest-tech stems from improvements to one (or more) of three capabilities:

- Data latency: how fast new data can be transmitted from its source to a receiving party

- Inferential depth: how rich or intricate of an analysis can be performed to generate fresh insights for decision making

- Resource efficiency: how productively organizational resources can be utilized, after accounting for the costs (e.g., time, money, oversight requirements) of that utilization

These are the core ingredients to advances all across invest-tech's history. When combined, they interact in potent—and typically predictable—ways. First, advances in invest-tech have a characteristic *burstiness*: they make pronounced, infrequent jumps forward along one (or, more rarely, both) of the first two dimensions, which are followed by gradual increases in efficiency. Thus, people tend to see "breakthrough" invest-tech as that which produces significant decreases in data latency or increases in inferential depth—despite the fact that improvements to efficiency regularly have stronger cumulative impacts on long-term performance.

Second, taking advantage of advances on one of these three dimensions oftentimes requires an organization to make sacrifices along the other two. For example, obtaining and acting on data more quickly (i.e., capitalizing on lower data latency) can compel an Investor to accept shallower inferences from that data, and potentially increase its total risk exposure.[4] Conversely, extracting deeper inferences—for example, untangling nuanced relationships between risk and return—can increase reaction times, which means forgoing some of the benefits from fast decision making after fresh data arrives.[5] Similarly, organizations usually must accept an *initial* dip in efficiency when adopting a novel technology (largely because their people, processes, and infrastructures will need some time to adjust to it). How long that dip lasts reflects how suitable that technology is for the organization's context at the time of adoption.

It is important to note, however, that there exists a characteristic asymmetry in trade-offs between the first two dimensions and the third. The initial decreases in efficiency that come from deepening inference or increasing speed tend to be *proportionally greater* than any immediate degradation of inferential depth or data latency that comes from enhancing efficiency. That is, the upfront hit to efficiency that results from improving inferences or speed is usually larger than any temporary drag on inferences or speed that's due to becoming more efficient. This asymmetry can be profoundly valuable to Investors, as we'll see in later chapters.

Whirlwind Tour

To kick off our historical tour, we must distinguish between invest-tech and financial technology (fin-tech). Invest-tech is a subset of fin-tech. Straightforwardly, invest-tech encompasses only technology that has to do with investing, whereas fin-tech covers all tech involved with finance (e.g., consumer banking). In light of recent media attention given to fin-tech, one might think it's mostly a new phenomenon. But fin-tech has actually been around for millennia. The abacus, limited-liability corporations, automated teller machines (ATMs), and even currency itself are all fin-tech. And, even though invest-tech's history stretches less far back than fin-tech's, it still spans several millennia.[6] It's also inseparable from the history of data in investing, because the two are heavily interdependent.

One of the earliest examples of invest-tech appeared in Mesopotamia, around 4000 BCE. Some astute ancient Babylonians noticed that changes in specific commodity prices were related to conditions of the Euphrates River, which affected both cultivation and transportation of those goods. To better track these relationships, a few shrewd individuals started using reed styluses to etch commodity prices (e.g., barley, dates, mustard, cardamom, sesame, and wool) in cuneiform script onto clay tablets, alongside depth and flow measurements of the Euphrates (Lo and Hasanhodzic 2010). These correlation records were probably the first instances of "spreadsheets." They increased the inferential depth that invest-tech could achieve—by virtue of helping merchants use data to better understand the joint dynamics of prices and physical phenomena.

Data latency was relatively unimportant in such early applications. Swings in commodity prices lagged sufficiently far behind changes in the Euphrates' conditions, and transactions were (in almost all cases) individually negotiated. As such, getting data quickly conferred few practical advantages. It sufficed for forward-thinking merchants to have just a little data on how observed conditions were likely to affect prices a few weeks or months ahead, so that they could make better stockpiling decisions.

Indeed, for much of history, the value of low data latency has been blunted by lack of well-organized markets and standardization.[7] In fact, over invest-tech's full history, low literacy and numeracy have been a far greater hindrance to its progress than data latency. Further, for most of history, investment-related data has needed to be recorded and maintained by hand. Therefore, historically, a greater concern than speed has been error detection (including catching inaccuracies due to fraud).

One of the biggest leaps forward in remedying that concern came during the fourteenth and fifteenth centuries from Italian city-states. The Genoese Treasury was among the first to use an accounts system that comprised columns of debits listed next to columns of credits (Lauwers and Willekens 1994). Such bilateral configurations for accounts meant that debits and credits could be efficiently paired, and thus any irregularities (whether honest mistakes or fraud) more readily identified. The Genoese system soon spread throughout the Italian peninsula, and was famously codified by a Franciscan friar, Luca Pacioli, in what today is called *double-entry bookkeeping* (Gleeson-White 2013).[8] Double-entry accounting was an advance not only in control over financial data: it also permitted efficient and deeper inferences on fundamental relationships (e.g., cash flows and asset-liability balances) that govern the health of businesses, institutions, and economies— both then and now.[9] Interestingly, it was shortly after the emergence of this new mode of accounting that data latency began to genuinely impede invest-tech's progress.

In 1602, the Dutch East India Company founded the Amsterdam Stock Exchange. While this wasn't the first-ever securities exchange (many exchanges in Europe and the Mediterranean, both formal and informal, pre-dated the one in Amsterdam), it was unprecedented in the volume of transactions it facilitated (Petram and Richards 2014). For the first time, enough liquidity existed in a single marketplace to convert traders' speed in acquiring data into valuable competitive edges. Soon thereafter, other large, formalized exchanges emerged. Still, progress in invest-tech across them all was restricted by a common constraint: the speed of *human* travel. As data and information still had to be exchanged interpersonally (i.e., with humans as messengers), data latency became a limiting factor, since data could travel only as fast as humans (e.g., carried via ship or horseback).

From the seventeenth to the mid-twentieth century, most progress in invest-tech (arguably) came from increasing the speed with which data reached decision makers: by removing *human* speed limits. A storied application of this involved the House of Rothschild capitalizing on the outcome of the Battle of Waterloo in 1815. The Rothschilds purportedly used carrier pigeons to relay news of Napoleon's defeat before it reached others in London's banking community. They then made a killing by buying gilts. And while historians have since established that the Rothschilds actually learned of the victory by nonavian means, they and others definitely used the speed advantages of winged messengers on many other occasions (Kay 2013). In any case, until the nineteenth century, data latency's lower bound was effectively set by windspeed.

In the 1830s–1840s, Samuel Morse and others developed the telegraph. After that, the limit of data latency became the speed of electricity. Notably, in 1867 (only one year after the first transatlantic telegraph cable became functional) the first telegraph-enabled stock-ticker machine was unveiled by Edward Calahan (it was refined by Thomas Edison in 1869) (Kirkpatrick and Dahlquist 2016). Data on securities prices could finally be transmitted over long distances in a miniscule amount of time, without need for trained telegraph operators (i.e., that knew Morse code) to transcribe them. With price data able to be automatically transmitted at very low latency, depth of inference became the primary bottleneck to progress in invest-tech. It has stayed so until today.

That's not to say that breakthroughs in inferential depth haven't occurred in the intervening decades. The invention of integrated circuits in the mid-twentieth century, and precipitous rise of digital computers ever since, has fully transformed the sophistication of insights that can be drawn from financial data (and vastly improved the efficiency with which many tasks are performed). Nay, the reason inferential depth is still the chief constraint on progress for invest-tech is that data latency has continued improving at a comparable (and very likely greater) rate—not only in terms of how fast data can reach investment decision makers, but also in the sheer volume that it does so.

Notably, the internet's birth caused a data deluge that exacerbates Investors' struggles to get a handle on invest-tech and derive comparative advantages from it (as opposed to having it be a persistent weakness). Data, in a global sense, is more accessible than ever. In lieu of clay slabs, touchscreen tablets now provide mobile access to vast troves of data that *should* be providing Investors with incomparable insight. But, problematically, (and as we explain shortly), Investors find it difficult to manage all this data and harvest deep, actionable inferences from it.

History's Takeaways

This DeLorean ride through invest-tech's history makes two points salient. The first is that there's an ordering on the durability of competitive advantages that can be gained by using new technologies. From the examples above (and also many others that we lack space to discuss), it's noticeable that any advantages based on speed will tend to have shorter shelf lives than those from inferential depth—in the respect that there tend to be fewer barriers to organizations accessing speed advantages (e.g., using carrier pigeons) than advantages from performing deeper inference (e.g., numeracy and computer savviness). Likewise, tech-enabled improvements to resource efficiency tend to hold their value longer than do those in inferential depth: one party possessing deeper understanding of risks and opportunities in a market makes others relatively less competitive; yet one organization becoming more cost-efficient through using new technology won't necessarily make others less so. If an organization uses new tech to gain deeper insights into its internal operations (for the sake of more efficiently using its own resources), then this advantage is not directly eroded by other organizations using that same technology. This hierarchy of durability in competitive advantages from data latency, inferential depth, and resource efficiency has strong implications for Investors. We study these in the chapters to come.

The second main takeaway from our tour is that, across history, the most transformational technologies in finance have originated from outside the investor community. This observation reinforces the idea that successful innovation comes as often from rediscovering existing solutions and finding creative ways to implement them in new domains as it does from inventing entirely new technology. This reality has serious import for any Investor that looks only to its peers (or other members of the financial community) for inspiration on innovation. Yet, our own research suggests most Investors are in fact doing just that. Investors need to break from this status quo and start widening their fields of vision in seeking technology. To underscore that point, for the rest of the book, we'll limit our use of the term *invest-tech*. We'll simply talk about *technology*.

The Tyranny of Spreadsheets

We next turn from the history of invest-tech in general to the specific problems Investors face from present-day technologies. Before doing so, however, we pause to consider why one technology emblematizes persistent problems faced by the financial community at large. That technology is the humble spreadsheet. Although seemingly mundane, it is in truth tyrannous.

Many financial organizations' relationships with spreadsheets can be neatly summarized by Thomas Jefferson's colorful statement: "But, as it is, we have the wolf by the ear, and we can neither hold him nor safely let him go." Of course, Mr. Jefferson was talking about slavery rather than Microsoft Excel. Nonetheless, the degree to which many financial institutions are dependent on spreadsheets is a grave issue. Most investment banks and asset managers rely on spreadsheets to store significant amounts of critical and sensitive data, as well as to perform mission-critical analyses. Although convenient (at least superficially), using spreadsheets for these purposes can be enormously limiting.[10] They hold back improvements from deeper inference and lower data latency. Spreadsheets perform poorly at dealing with large-volume data, severely restrict the types of analyses that can be performed, and—without some fancy additional coding—are largely limited to static data, which must be refreshed manually to reflect updated information.[11]

Even with the above shortcomings, spreadsheets are today one of the mostly widely used technologies in finance. They are so entrenched within organizations that most find it hard to "quit spreadsheets," despite their sincere desire to do so. This addiction is harmful, not only because it bogs down progress in inferential technology: it also exposes organizations to many potential risks that are often hard to detect or combat. It turns out that many of these same risks pervade other incumbent technologies used by Investors. As such, spreadsheets serve as a useful showcase for raising these problems, which include:

- Zombies: because spreadsheets are mostly saved to local drives on users' machines, there's a real risk of obsolete, possibly error-filled copies persisting in an organization, which can lead to misinformed decision making. Finding and purging these zombie files can be tough (but hey, dealing with zombies is in the job description for superheroes!).

- Tracing: relatedly, the newest version of a spreadsheet can often be hard to track down unless an organization has a centralized mechanism for disseminating it. Similarly, a user may easily come to possess a spreadsheet of unknown origin, which makes it difficult to trace its provenance (e.g., to know if it can be trusted, or where to go to ask questions about it).

- Opacity: aside from tracing a spreadsheet's origin, knowing where the data in it came from can be a challenge unless users who entered that data fastidiously document the sources they used. This opacity in data sources creates obstacles for efficiently verifying data's accuracy.

- Error propagation: spreadsheets usually combine many discrete, interlinked calculations that are spread across different cells or sheets in a workbook (or, worse still, portaged between one workbook and another). This setup makes error checking a time-gobbling, albeit necessary, task: an upstream error can become compounded as it flows through downstream calculations.

- Bandaging: the flexibility of spreadsheets means that it's often easier for a user to come up with a quick-and-dirty workaround rather than develop a solution that will remain time-saving and reliable in the future. But, these "bandages" tend to persist once created, and so leave the problems that cause them unaddressed.

Combatting these challenges can be effortful for organizations, but the potential pitfalls of spreadsheets don't stop there. Spreadsheets can also exacerbate many human biases, while also hiding them from others. That is, conventional methods and layouts for building spreadsheets can push their authors to engage in biased thinking, such as:

- Focusing too much on upside or downside cases

- Not looking enough at the long term (e.g., thinking about just the columns that fit on-screen, as time is usually represented from left-to-right or top-to-bottom in a sheet)

- Enticing people to shoehorn ambiguity and uncertainty into a single number, which can conceal from other users just how unsure they are about values they've entered

- Narrowly thinking that (per Kahneman [2011]) "What you see is all there is"

The advanced technologies that we study in coming chapters offer a chance to escape this tyranny, provided that Investors are motivated to kick their spreadsheet habit for good (as they should be!).

CHAPTER 2 TECHNOLOGY PROBLEMS IN INSTITUTIONAL INVESTING

Toward Entrenched Advantages

Here, we undertake a deep dive into the current state of technology across the Investor community. Our findings are disheartening, if unsurprising. Broadly, our research finds that Investors' operations, and thereby long-term performances, are hamstrung by tech-related troubles. Our work has identified ten specific problems at the root of Investors' tech woes, which we describe below. We dub these problems "entangling," since they aren't hardships caused by technology alone, and so cannot be fixed solely with technology. Rather, they're problems partly caused by the structural, cultural, and governance factors behind how Investors function. This realization may at first seem like a reason for despair. If Investors' tech problems are so deep seated, then is technologizing worth all the effort? On the surface, it's tempting to think not.

But it's precisely this sort of knee-jerk thinking that can cause one to overlook the truly transformative, game-changing opportunity: entangling problems are challenging but needn't be permanent. In addressing them, Investors could reverse their relationship with tech and turn it from a weakness into an enduring strength, in other words, convert entangling problems into entrenched advantages that are reinforced by technologically enhanced governance, culture, and strategic planning. Doing this would give Investors self-strengthening superpowers! As we'll see, achieving this change isn't as daunting a task as one might at first suspect. The emergence of new technological paradigms (which we'll cover in the next chapter) will help clear a path for Investors in reorienting themselves around technology for their long-term success.

Common Scapegoats

Without doubt, entangling problems are the main obstacles Investors face in technologizing. Nevertheless, several other hurdles garner most of the blame for Investors' tech conundrums. Luckily, these scapegoat problems are usually easier for Investors to resolve than their entangling problems are.

The first scapegoat problem is cost. A common reason we hear for Investors' tech troubles is that high-performing technology is prohibitively expensive. It's inarguable that technology can be pricey. Yet, in a global sense, it's cheap! Investors routinely spend an *entire order of magnitude* more on fees (paid to external managers and consultants) than they do on their own technology. If some of those fee outlays were diverted to technologizing, then Investors could easily afford the best investment technology available. Tech is mainly "costly" because spending is misallocated.

The irony in blaming cost for not being able to afford to technology is that this creates other costs for Investors: opportunity costs. One major pension fund we've studied—which is one of the premier Investors globally in terms of how well it manages its data—estimates it could boost its returns by about 100 basis points annually if it were able to fully modernize its data-management and governance systems.[1] Mind you, that extra 1 percent in return would be a *pure* 1 percent: it'd be largely risk-free and, as calculated, be net of costs for upgrading. For Investors whose data systems are less matured than that leading Investor's, the boost to returns could be far higher. The assumption that top technology is prohibitively costly should be replaced by a question: How could Investors legitimately afford to *not* access the benefits from using better tech?

Another popular scapegoat is outsourcing. We hear—time and again—that many external asset managers and consultants have comparative advantages when it comes to technology, and so Investors should let *them* handle new tech, rather than Investors building or expanding their own internal capacities for technology. It's true that it can be efficient and cost-effective to let those parties absorb some of Investors' technology needs (e.g., by letting them take on a bit of the risk in figuring out how to deploy untested technologies for new applications). However, Investors shouldn't rely on external parties to the extent our research finds they do. By depending on other parties for the lion's share of their access to technology, Investors incur hefty costs that compound over time. Hence, Investors end up subsidizing other parties' technology advantages.[2] In doing so, Investors forgo serious long-term benefits they could have reaped from cultivating their own capabilities. Doing so also deepens Investors' reliance on external parties, and implicitly commits them to paying exorbitant, unjustified fees for the long haul. By outsourcing tech capacity, Investors reduce their opportunity sets and end up mortgaging their net returns.

A final scapegoat comes via the argument that it's ideal to be a "close follower" in embracing advanced tech. The logic for this assertion is that it's optimal to let others tackle risks associated with new tech, and then cherry-pick technologies that ultimately prove successful. To us, this stance feels like an artful way of condoning herding behavior. Just emulating others is a flawed strategy. It can cause an Investor to look too narrowly for best-fit technologies: it restricts their option set to what's tried by their peers, which is only a small subset of potential solutions. This problem worsens when one realizes that technologies that work well for one organization needn't be fit for others. Success in one organizational context doesn't translate into success elsewhere, since there are inherent idiosyncrasies in all Investor's organizations.[3] Finally, the benefits of a successful technology can sometimes take time to become visible or measurable—especially to outside organizations. By the time they actually surface, many advantages (maybe durable ones) that could've been claimed by early adoption will likely have evaporated.[4]

For these reasons, we advise that, in weighing and formulating their own strategies for technologizing, Investors look past the above distractors and instead focus on entangling problems.

Entangling Problems

The rest of this chapter is devoted to identifying and dissecting ten entangling problems that hold Investors back, not just from technologizing, but from even using their current tech to decent effect. These are:

- Silos and fragmentation
- Wrong focal scales
- Poor measurement
- No first-class citizenship
- Deprioritized innovation
- Untrustworthy data
- Complexity-agility imbalance
- Isolated perspectives
- Weak cooperativity and collectivism
- Misunderstood data edges

Essentially all of Investors' specific problems with technology are directly traceable to these ten problems. Although we treat each one of these in turn, it's imperative to see that any one of them can worsen the others. This reality is actually good news for Investors! It means tackling even one of these is likely to alleviate some of the other nine. We'll explore how to do so in coming chapters.

Silos and Fragmentation

Fragmented organizational structure is one of the thorniest barriers to effectively using technology. Siloed structures result in coordination problems, which are especially pernicious for technology because of the incompatibilities, gaps, and opacities that siloes create. Many of the benefits that technology can deliver to an organization come from an increased ability to share, integrate, and access data, information, and knowledge. But siloed organizations create frictions on these abilities because they regularly cause breakdowns in communication. Such breakdowns nullify attempts to make usage of technology *consistent*, *efficient*, and *empowering* across the organization.

These frictions are also worsened by the blockages that silos create for monitoring-and-feedback loops. Constipated feedback loops make it hard for those in the organization who are in charge of technology to recognize

- whether users are productively leveraging the technology available to them,

- if users may be better served by different technologies, and

- whether users are aware of the technologies that are already available to them in the organization, and how to most efficiently use those.

On the flipside, siloed organizations make it harder for users to

- share best-practices on technology with one another, and

- offer suggestions or requests to decision makers who handle the organization's technology resources.

These impediments from fragmentation have further knock-on effects in both technology and organizational function. First, they obstruct attempts at "whole-fund" visibility. Many Investors are actively engaged in efforts to better understand their portfolios from bottom to top. But siloed structures can thwart those efforts, as they make information flows between different parts of an organization viscous and inconsistent. Partial, inconsistent availability of information means technologies that use information cannot operate at their full potentials, which distorts their value for the organization (in the downward direction). Second, fragmentation oftentimes leads to cultural divisions and heterogeneity. These mean that different areas of the organization may draw different conclusions despite using the same data technology,

which could erode coordinated and aligned understanding and decision making. One senior practitioner voiced this concern as: "How can
we have faith that, even when we are saying the same thing, what we
mean is truly the same?"

Wrong Focal Scales

A second entangling problem Investors face on technology is due to the
scales on which they focus. When searching for, examining, and planning to implement technologies that improve operations and
investment-management functions, Investors tend to THINK BIG and
prioritize solutions that promise large-scale change (which is often
conflated with *big gains*). Big projects routinely receive undue attention
and resources relative to smaller ones, even when the latter have proportionally greater benefits. While extensive change is needed in many
Investors' tech capabilities, it doesn't follow that these changes should
all take the form of megaprojects. Indeed, going big is often antithetical
to nimbleness, which (as we elaborate on later) is required for ongoing
innovation.

The tendency to think about technology, and technological change,
on large scales is also problematic when it comes to project evaluation.
Our studies find that

- investors regularly try hard to find "win-win" opportunities in
  tech projects, even though such projects almost always entail tradeoffs (win-wins are rare),[5] and

- investors are biased toward emphasizing tech projects' short-term
  effects on investment returns, with less consideration given to
  long-term impacts.[6]

In conjunction with a win-win fixation, overstressing gross near-term
returns can tempt Investors into spending more time exploring large
projects that are actually riskier than portfolios of small, long-term
projects (each of which may have a small impact on gross returns, but
can be cheaper and less risky to implement—and, in aggregate, result
in a better risk-adjusted outcome than a single massive project). This

temptation is worrying, given how large-scale projects more regularly incur time and cost overruns than smaller ones do.

Poor Measurement

Another entangling problem related to overemphasis of big scales is the measurement challenges that Investors face in assessing technology. That is, Investors are harmed by a paucity of consistent, rigorous methods for

- analyzing technology that has uncertain benefits and costs (this applies to both technologies they already possess, as well as new ones),
- determining how efficiently they are using their data, and
- measuring where within their organization technology changes will yield the most long-term value.

Investors aren't entirely at fault for this lack of measurement tools. The financial-services industry at large is plagued by the same shortage. That said, Investors are directly and negatively affected by it in at least three ways. First, it can compel them to excessively favor projects that have clear benefits and costs over those that may have less certain upsides and downsides—even when there may be reason to believe that the net value of more uncertain projects may be higher under a majority of likely outcomes.[7] Second, when there is uncertainty, benefits and costs are usually treated unequally: expected benefits tend to be diluted down, while expected costs tend to get pushed up. Although this might be written off as reflecting *conservatism*, the degree to which we observe it happen—especially in the evaluation of data—convinces us that it's being injudiciously practiced. Finally, the absence of solid measurement systems promotes short-termism. By and large, the short term is clearer than the long term, which can make projects that deliver near-term outcomes more enticing than ones that provide benefits over the longer term, even though favoring the short term makes little sense for long-term organizations.

    In total, a shortage of sound diagnostics on the performance of technologies and data (and ways to judge these ex ante) helps perpetuate unhealthy perspectives among Investors about what technologies, and tech projects, are worthwhile.

No First-Class Citizenship

Investment technology often fails to get treated like a first-class citizen in Investors' organizations. We've already alluded to the fact that technology is routinely seen more as a cost sink than an advantage generator (as is indicated by how much is spent on it compared with the fees Investors pay to third parties). This often makes tech "late to dinner" in receiving its due share of budgetary resources. This bias of accentuating technology's costs has made starvation diets for tech popular among Investors: they give their own tech enough resources to allow the organization to scrape by (at least in the near term), but never enough to let it attain its full potential. This second-class citizenship isn't limited to funding; it's also evident in the lack of top-level visibility given to tech. In many organizations, there isn't a chief *technology* officer or equivalent role. Where these do exist, their responsibilities are frequently folded in with those of other functions, for example, overall operations. Moreover, technology teams in Investors' organizations are often underresourced (i.e., understaffed and overworked) and cloistered away as support functions—not embedded within each unit of the organization. Given this lack of first-class citizenship, it's little wonder why few Investors feel that they can't build and sustain durable competitive advantages through technology.

Deprioritized Innovation

Even where technology isn't relegated to lower-class citizenship, its contributions to innovation are typically underprioritized. Rather than being configured to help Investors "surf the big ones," their tech—and systems and processes for supporting it—is more oriented to tread water (i.e., maintain existing functions and processes rather than innovate to develop new capabilities). Like technology, innovation lacks first-class citizenship in most Investors' organizations.[8] Innovation is mostly treated as a nebulous construct—something nice to have, but for which no formal protocols, budgets, or teams exist. Given this ad-hoc nature, it's no shock that innovation also routinely gets starved of resources in Investors' organizations. And it's hard for something with such inconsistent treatment to yield consistent results (which, in a perverse circularity, is often cited as a reason not to devote more resources toward innovating: it's putatively too "unreliable"). But consistency is exactly what's needed for innovation to succeed!

To some readers, consistency and innovation may seem strange bedfellows. After all, isn't innovation a result of things like inspiration and serendipity? Yes, but only to a very minor degree. *Consistent innovation* is actually more of a methodical science than an art (we'll unpack that in a later chapter). It requires purposefully allocated resources, well-defined processes for experimentation, and effective dissemination mechanisms to share results across the organization. These are absent as norms among Investors, which hinders their success with tech. Pointedly, technology without innovation is almost always inefficient: it leaves much of technology's (context-specific) potential untapped. Similarly, innovation without tech is largely incomplete, due to not being pushed far enough. To succeed in reorienting their organizations around tech, Investors have to prioritize innovation.

Untrustworthy Data

Investors are plagued by untrustworthy data. This entangling problem is due to a need to improve their data-management and governance systems, as well as resolve inadequacies in organizations with whom they partner (e.g., many custodians and data vendors). Sound data is at the heart of sound decision making. And decision making is the very soul of what any Investor does. Hence, untrustworthy data threatens the entire undertaking of institutional investing.

Nonetheless, it persists. Admittedly, designing and implementing systems that effectively manage and govern data across an organization is no small feat. But doing so is vital if Investors' are to successfully technologize. Bluntly, most advanced technology is data related: it either produces valuable data, relies on data inputs, or does both. Crummy data kneecaps technology.

Investors struggle with their data in various ways. They have a hard time: (1) making sure responsibility for governance and management of any particular data set is assigned to a specific individual in the organization; and (2) ensuring those individuals are properly executing their responsibilities as stewards of data (including purging old or bad data from the organization). They also struggle with ensuring that data is *consistent* across their organization—in other words (and as we've heard it colorfully phrased), "Multiple versions of 'the truth' don't exist simultaneously." And they struggle to maintain control of their data, and make sure it stays inside organizational boundaries (when it needs to) and isn't unduly vulnerable.

Complexity-Agility Imbalance

Investors persistently grapple with striking a suitable balance between the *complexity* and *agility* of their tech resources (and processes for managing them). This is an intricate problem, due to the fact that complexity and agility have a nonlinear relationship. Having a suite of technologies that is complex (i.e., many different technologies that are interconnected in nontrivial ways) can limit how agile an organization is. On the other hand, organizations with oversimplified, monolithic tech platforms may also struggle with agility, as switching to other platforms or adding new capabilities may be prohibitively effortful.

But this complexity-agility balance must be struck not only in an Investor's technology mix itself: it also has to be achieved in how an Investor's people and process resources interact with its tech—for example, through governance or cultural channels. Managing this balance at the level of people is an especially crucial function, and entails deciding how much decision-making capacity to delegate to individuals, teams, and divisions within the organization. Finding ways to identify this balance is imperative for technologizing. We cover them extensively in later chapters.

Isolated Perspectives

A consistent finding in our investigations is that Investors' perspectives on the overall landscape for technology (invest-tech and otherwise) is significantly local and isolated. For the most part, there is scant understanding of what their peers are doing from a technology stand-point, for example, what tools they're using, how they choose them, what struggles and victories they encounter in their sourcing and implementation processes, what's on their "tech radar," and what their plans are for the future. More broadly, many Investors are not well-apprised about emerging technologies in general (including deep learning, blockchain, alternative data, etc.). Lack of wider awareness is a genuine problem for Investors that'll hamper their success in technologizing. Part of taking a wider view will necessarily involve more extensive interaction with start-up communities and new entities entering into the investment domain from outside of finance. Right now, almost no Investors have well-calibrated processes (or even blueprints) for doing so.[9]

Weak Cooperativity and Collectivism

Apart from communicating too little with one another about technology, Investors rarely cooperate on working with technology (let alone codeveloping it). Despite the reality that many Investors aren't really competitors—or are only very indirectly so—joint efforts to combine resources and create better tech outcomes are scarce (and border on nonexistence). This is wasteful. Individually, Investors can achieve fantastic outcomes from technologizing. But, by banding together, changes they could generate would be *revolutionary*. As we've already noted, if Investors could pool some of their resources toward technology (without even needing to significantly change their budgets—they'd simply need to divert some spending away from external managers' fees), they would easily have the same capital resources to unleash on innovation as do Google, Microsoft, Apple, and so on. But it's not just an absence of pooled resources in tech innovation that's holding Investors back from achieving tech success. They're also failing to act collectively in demanding more fit-for-purpose solutions from intermediaries, such as custodians and incumbent technology vendors. Cooperation and collectivism are potentially the greatest untapped resource Investors have overall.

Misunderstood Data Edges

The final entangling problem that causes technological suffering for Investors is the need to more comprehensively understand their latent "edges" when it comes to data. The data capabilities Investors do target oftentimes don't play to their strengths as long-term asset owners. For instance, many Investors wrongly prioritize data about liquid, public markets, where building comparative advantages is costly and requires continual reinvestment to stay even remotely competitive. *All* Investors, however, have a competitive edge in one form of data that isn't available to others (even their peers): their own internal data. We find few Investors are taking sufficient advantage of this resource to generate meaningful *operational alpha* from novel forms of data on their own organizations—in terms of their processes, networks, and people. Not emphasizing or harvesting the value of this data discourages many Investors from looking more seriously at technologies that could help them take better advantage of this native and unassailable edge, which is available to every Investor. Apart from data they already possess but don't use, we also find many Investors aren't thinking enough about how they can acquire new forms of data—specifically from new sources that could form the basis of long-horizon capabilities that other organizations couldn't threaten. That is, Investors aren't looking into how they could create "defensible" data strategies.[10]

Toward a Best-Fit Toolkit

In the next two chapters, we build a toolkit to help Investors tackle these entangling problems and find ways to turn them from weaknesses into sources of strength for the journey of technologizing. In assembling this toolkit, we'll first look at the current trajectory of emerging technologies that are relevant to Investors. Then, we'll construct best-fit frameworks to help Investors assess them.

CHAPTER 3 TECHNOLOGY TRENDS AND TOOLS

Outfitting the Technologized Investor

It almost goes without saying: for a successful mission, any would-be tech superhero must be well equipped with the right supergadgetry. In this chapter, we discuss the best candidates to stock Investors' superhero toolbelts. Then, in the next chapter, we'll cover frameworks for Investors to use in evaluating and choosing tools for their respective missions. Remember, no tech superhero can afford being laden down with underperforming gadgets. Knowing what advanced technology is available—and how to select best-fit solutions—can itself be a superpower for many Investors.

To see what advanced technologies Investors may leverage in their missions, and directions in which these new solutions are headed, it's helpful to understand the broader backdrop against which they're evolving. That'll allow us to more firmly grasp the main categories of cutting-edge technology that Investors can use to supercharge their organizations.

Currents of Technological Change

The twentieth century was utterly dominated by technology. It transformed the jobs we do, the food we eat, the healthcare we receive, how we communicate, how we travel, how we wage war, how we're entertained, and most other aspects of our modern lives. The blistering pace of this tech-fueled transformation shows absolutely no sign of slowing in the current century. The most significant accelerators of change in the twenty-first century were, however, relatively late arrivals during the twentieth. They are—with little surprise—the digital computer and internet. Although the first genuine computer was born during World War II (largely from ideas cultivated by Alan Turing), it wasn't until the 1980s that this invention got traction in wider society and began having substantial social and economic impact. Nor was it until the last months of the previous millennium that the internet began its ascendance as one of the defining forces in daily life.

We've seen how inferential depth and data latency (along with resource efficiency) have been hallmarks of invest-tech's progress throughout history. Unsurprisingly, increasing inferential depth and declining data latency are also key forces behind the current cutting-edge tech to which computers and the internet have given rise.

Indeed, Moore's law and the explosion of data produced by our internet-connected lives are together remaking humankind's reality.[1] The tandem of ever-more-powerful data-processing capabilities and surging volume, diversity, and speed of computing-generated data is leading to almost unfathomable inferential depth and low-latency data.[2] Inferential depth and data latency are now locked in a mutually accelerating dance that is spawning entirely new fields of technology at what feels like an impossible clip.

Yet, it isn't trends in inferential depth and data latency alone that give the best indication of where advanced technologies are headed (at least in the foreseeable future): the pervasive impact of these two forces makes them more helpfully seen as *macrotrends* in the ongoing progress of technology. *Simplicity* and *openness* of cutting-edge technology are perhaps the most useful trends for reading the tech tea leaves. By simplicity, we don't mean that cutting-edge technologies lack complexity. Rather, they're generally growing simpler *for users*. Pleasing, straightforward user experiences (UXs) characterize today's dominant technologies.[3] More and more technologies are simple to use, in an out-of-the-box, plug-and-play manner (i.e., "batteries included").

Advanced technologies are also becoming increasingly *open* in several ways (Monk and Rook 2018). For one, many technologies now function inside open ecosystems. Take iOS and Android operating systems for smartphones, tablets, and so forth. Most apps that those systems support aren't built by Apple or Google, but by outside developers who use those platforms as hosts for their own software. This aspect of openness is far reaching and showing up in diverse forms, such as new blockchain platforms and the intercompatibility of many popular tools in artificial intelligence. The open-ecosystem trend has been boosted by another dimension of openness in technology: open-source code. A rising number of the most popular and powerful software tools today are based on publicly accessible and modifiable code.[4] The open-sourcing of software has boosted open ecosystems' impact by allowing many tools to be significantly interoperable (e.g., Android is based on an open-source software kernel). The open-sourcing trend also enables developers and engineers to straightforwardly inspect one another's creations, which is helping accelerate iterative software improvements.

A third stripe of openness is more open availability of high-performance computing, for example, cloud-based processing. Scrapping the need to physically own hardware has reduced or eliminated many previous barriers to affordable, large-scale processing and let new players directly participate in pushing forward the boundaries of digital technology. In turn, expanded access to computing is helped by a fourth dimension of openness: open learning. Today, an astonishing amount of high-quality resources are publicly and freely available to help would-be contributors to the advanced-technology boom build their knowledge and skills as software engineers, cybersecurity analysts, digital-systems architects, UX designers, data and computer scientists, and a smorgasbord of other roles. These open-learning resources are produced by both established institutions (e.g., Stanford, MIT, Harvard) and newer entities (e.g., Coursera, Udacity, Udemy), along with offerings available as blogs (e.g., on Medium), online tutorials via YouTube, and many other formats.

Regrettably, despite the momentum behind simplicity and openness, these trends haven't made significant landfall among the *incumbent* technologies most Investors use, that is, legacy technologies that many Investors have relied on for years and that have been built and sold by vendors who have too few incentives to seriously innovate. Those incumbent "solutions" largely remain stuck in a morass of stale technological paradigms, such as proprietary software and closed ecosystems (i.e., noninteroperable platforms).

Still, Investors shouldn't lose heart. They need to broaden their search horizons beyond the usual suspects—to look for novel technologies and partners to deliver them. Broadening those horizons, and giving a curated tour of them, is what the rest of this book ultimately does. We'll see exactly what superpowers Investors can acquire from various technologies—both already available and embryonic. To preview the flavor of what we'll encounter, we peer below at four broad classes of advanced tech tools that can make a powerful, immediate impact for Investors. But this is just a light sampling—an amuse-bouche. We'll take more substantial bites in chapters to come.

Artificial Intelligence

There's one advanced technology that—far more than any other—makes Investors we've studied simultaneously excited and unsettled: artificial intelligence (AI). Their reserved enthusiasm is both understandable and justifiable. AI's recent superhuman accomplishments suggest it could fast-track Investors' own tech superhero-hood. It's already besting doctors in making clinical diagnoses, beating the world's top players in hypercomplex games like go, outpredicting design gurus in anticipating emerging fashions, solving scientific puzzles that have baffled researchers for decades, writing some AI algorithms that are better than what top AI researchers can, and generally pulling off new, deeply impressive, highly publicized feats with each passing month.[5]

Still, AI also has its detractors. Voices both inside and outside the AI research community (notably, Elon Musk and the late Stephen Hawking) warn us of its perils—whether as a weapon for economic or military supremacy, or as an existential threat to human civilization.[6] Similarly, there are some who claim that the low-hanging fruit in AI's progress has been picked and that future advances will be more incremental and farther between.

We sit on the side of the measured optimists. We see the enormous power in AI that remains untapped; but we know its future progress may not always be as rapid and smooth as it's been for the past decade. That said, whatever the next phase of AI might hold, there's an astonishing array of AI technology available today that Investors have yet to recognize or incorporate into their own organizations. This ripe-but-unpicked tech can help Investors in two ways: (1) increasing the depth of inferences they're able to make, and (2) automating tasks that are repetitive, or for which human involvement doesn't add much value. That is, the judicious application of AI can expand Investors' in-house resources by increasing their effective expertise, information quality, and time efficiency.

Our interviews with Investors have revealed that three speedbumps act as the greatest deterrents to more widespread, extensive adoption of AI among institutional investors:

1. Confusion due to the perceived complexity of AI

2. Belief that AI is largely inaccessible without internal teams of experts

3. Difficulty of using AI without having the organization's data under control

Our own work with AI technology, however, suggests there really aren't three barriers—there's only half of one. Let us explain. First, AI is undeniably complicated if one wants to dive into the nitty-gritty details. But modern AI tools are actually pretty approachable and simple to grok if viewed from a high level (see Appendix). This brings us to the second realization: Investors can use some potent AI tools without needing a phalanx of computer-science PhDs on their payrolls. The only real prerequisite nowadays is having a few people with modest amounts of quantitative skill and the willingness to spend a little time iteratively improving solutions (i.e., fine-tuning AI models).[7] Tech organizations of all sizes (e.g., biggies like Facebook, Google, Uber, and

Salesforce, as well as smaller, newer outfits such as H2o.AI, Fast.AI, and OpenAI) are releasing and continually updating straightforward-to-use platforms that let users unleash AI on the sorts of real-world problems that are relevant for Investors.[8]

Finally, there's the data hurdle. We're not going to sugarcoat it: Investors who don't have their data management and data governance systems in good order won't get nearly as much bang for their AI buck as their peers who've gotten their data systems comfortably in check. Now, that doesn't mean *data perfection*. It means getting a handle on the quality of, and control over, data flows on which AI could be deployed (although having this be true for more organizational data means a wider, deeper reach in how an Investor can use AI). Moreover, there are other senses in which messy data is only a partial barrier to AI use among Investors. The two most consequential of these are the facts that

- new data sets of potential interest for AI applications are often available as-a-service, delivered through a subscription in a format that makes the data (nearly) immediately usable for AI purposes; and

- fresh forms of AI are emerging that rely as much on Investors' knowledge as on their data, thereby allowing them to make use of AI without needing to have first "solved" their data systems.

We'll be addressing both of these opportunities throughout the rest of the book. Right now, what readers should see is that there are many different *levels* at which an Investor can use AI in its processes—regardless of whether those processes are for investing or other (internal) operations. Some Investors might wish to reorient their organizations around not technology at large, but instead around AI in specific. In doing so, they could reap enormous benefits from a sound understanding and dexterous use of AI.[9] But Investors can also successfully technologize (as we expect most will) by having AI only be a fraction of their advanced-technology armament, not the centerpiece of it. In the rest of the book, we try to express our insights and suggestions so that they're valuable to Investors on both ends of this spectrum, as neither is inherently better or worse for Investors in general: what's right depends on each Investor's context. Regardless, we're guessing many readers might like to know a bit more about modern AI at a high level, especially if they haven't delved into it before. Thus, in the Appendix we give a concise flyover of current AI technology that'll have readers able to carry out at least a casual conversation on the topic.

Before moving on, there's a matter of terminology we must raise. Much of AI hinges on technology that is able to perform *inferences*. But AI algorithms aren't the only set of technology tools capable of making mathematical or logical inferences from data. In the rest of the book, we'll often refer to the wider class of tools that perform sophisticated inferences as *advanced-inference algorithms*. (This wider class of algorithms includes AI; but when we're specifically talking about AI—or a particular type thereof—we'll explicitly say so.)

Big and Alternative Data

We're unsure what's harder to avoid these days: chatter on AI or on big data. In the global financial community, symptoms of big-data fever have been around for longer than those for AI—although it can be argued that the financial world's infatuation with big data is merely an extension of its hunger for data in general. Now, there's increasing mention of another type of data among Investors: *alternative data* (alt-data).

Although alt-data intersects heavily with big data, the two don't perfectly overlap, and one isn't just a subset of the other. Big data is any data set that's of abnormally large size. For example, for some Investors, multiyear records of second-by-second prices in stock markets constitute big data (versus the more usual records of closing prices). Those records wouldn't, however, be alt-data, which we define as any data that *isn't conventionally used in investment decision making.*[10]

Examples of alt-data may include

- satellite imagery of commercial or economic activity (e.g., numbers of cars in retailers' parking lots, ships moored in ports, and farming or mining activities);

- social media, via which consumer, political, or other sentiment may be gauged;

- microdata on consumers' shopping activities (e.g., credit card transactions or in-app purchases on smartphones);

- data scraped from the internet (e.g., job postings to track hiring patterns);

- data exhaust—the assortment of log files, cookies, and other digital footprints created by people's online browsing (including geolocation data from searches on mobile devices).[11]

Alt-data sets, along with sensing and other technologies to capture and process them, are becoming magnetic for Investors. They're attracting mounting interest from Investors because they enlarge the sets of variables on which decisions can be based—for instance in identifying risk or fresh opportunities. Elsewhere, we've cautioned Investors against being lured into an "arms race" for alt-data (Monk, Prins, and Rook 2019). They must be wary of alt-data sets that invite short-termism. And they need to avoid chasing after and paying for data sets just to keep up with other market players.[12] Getting embroiled in such a race doesn't leverage Investors' long-term strengths.

Instead, we see alt-data as brimful of value for Investors in three ways. First, it can help Investors better understand risk, rather than merely trying to (weakly) measure it with basic statistics, such as volatility and correlations in asset prices. We'll have lots to say on this use for alt-data throughout the rest of the book. Second, alt-data can help Investors to more efficiently and effectively monitor and manage assets in their portfolio without transacting. For example, if an Investor has a direct equity position in a real-estate project at a remote location, then imagery (whether satellite photos or on-site video) that shows up-to-date construction progress can help it make sounder decisions, like: what it communicates with the project's manager; when to release more financing; or whether to seek input from outside experts (and ditch the current manager).

Third, we believe that perhaps the most valuable source and use for alt-data is an Investor's own in-house operations. Every Investor sits on troves of data, such as that buried in email chains, investment memos, pitch materials, spreadsheets stored on local drives, and a staggering diversity of other data generated from its internal processes. Most Investors make very little use of this data. It's therefore alt-data, because it's not methodically or consistently used for investment decisions.

We think this internal alt-data can be converted into hugely powerful sources of operating alpha—risk-free additions to net returns that come from improvements to operating efficiency. And there's another reason internal alt-data is a high-octane advantage for any Investor: other entities usually can't access it or make effective use of it, which means it's an unassailable resource that only the Investor who created it can tap (and absolutely should tap!).

There's a mushrooming number of ways and sources by which Investors can get access to noninternal alt-data, such as

- downloading or purchasing alt-data sets directly from third-party sources;

- using specialized platforms (e.g., Neudata) that curate various alt-data sets;

- subscribing to alt-data sets or alt-data-feeds on existing platforms (e.g., FactSet or Bloomberg);

- using platforms that prioritize delivery of insights from alt-data, rather than the provision of alt-data itself (e.g., Predata, which aggregates and analyzes social-media data to create hyperfocused, predictive risk indicators for users).

It's unlikely that a single source will fulfill an Investor's every need when it comes to noninternal alt-data. Hence, a mixture of the above sources is likely to make up any Investor's alt-data portfolio for the future.

One thing we must quickly point out before moving on is the symbiosis between alt-data and AI. The majority of modern AI tools need (large volumes of) specialized data to deliver high-powered insights, whereas many alt-data sets need AI to make sense of their own complexity. It's true that there's plenty of alt-data that isn't big data and is readily interpretable by humans (even ones without killer math skills). However, we expect the sharpest gains in the depth of inferences Investors can make will come from combining alt-data and AI in creative new ways.

Collaboration Utilities

AI and alt-data tools may be the sexiest advanced tech on a technologized Investor's toolbelt, but they aren't universally the most valuable solutions. Our research suggests tools that allow more sophisticated collaboration—both inside Investors' organizations and with parties outside them—might yield at least as much value in the future as AI and alt-data do. We've always found it curious (and aggravating) that, although Investors' essential roles are as responsible decision makers, their organizations aren't well positioned for (even internal) collaboration—despite the fact that most of the important decisions they make are not down to one individual alone. They're collaborative!

Discoordinated or otherwise inefficient communication is an obstacle that Investors in our research have cited—many, many times—as blocking them from embracing top technologies. Sound communication is central to fluid collaboration, but many of the standard communication tools Investors use don't let information *flow* as it needs to. Nor do they really lend themselves to *iterative* (i.e., back-and-forth) exchanges of information that are vital to productive innovation (we'll cover why that's so in later chapters). Bloated inboxes of email threads that knot together like yarn, point-to-point circulation of spreadsheets, and unannotated analyses that seem to materialize out of thin air aren't building blocks for empowering collaboration or communication.

Technologized Investors can do better. And some already are. We've noticed a small cadre of enterprising Investors that are embracing next-generation collaboration technologies, with some very positive results thus far. Solutions they're using include the following.

- **Repositories for sharing and coworking** on documents, models, and other files that allow strong version control, user annotation, and capabilities for merging and splitting projects. Implementations like private GitHub accounts are prime examples.[13]

- **Integrated and flexible communication platforms** like Slack that are designed to be highly searchable.[14] Project-management and connectivity tools of this stripe are rapidly coming to fit more niches that are relevant for Investors (e.g., utilities like Trello, Discord, and JIRA).

- **Analytical canvases that facilitate documentation** like Jupyter Notebooks or Google Colab, which can put analysts' and other contributors' notes in highly visible locations in the same document and easily include rich links to original materials (or directly embed those materials themselves).

Collaboration tech is fast becoming more seamless within organizations. It'll be even more so as AI and alt-data (specifically, alt-data produced by collaborative activities themselves) increasingly enter the feedback loop and improve collaboration and communication on-the-fly.

There are also astounding new technologies that are augmenting collaboration possibilities with entities outside an Investor's organizational borders. We believe two in particular could play pivotal roles in transforming how Investors collaborate with parties beyond their organizations. A first set of technologies revolve around encryption. There are many cases where an Investor may be keen to collaborate with another party, but the basis for that collaboration isn't directly sharable—for example, a sensitive or proprietary data set. Advanced encryption technology is enabling collaboration in such cases by allowing Investors to work on shared resources when they don't have direct access to them. Inpher, for instance, provides a tool set that allows one party to perform sophisticated analyses on another party's data, without ever accessing the underlying data or being able to reconstruct it.[15]

A second set of technologies for extraorganizational collaboration involves decentralized prediction markets. Crowd wisdom is by now a well-documented phenomenon, but until recently setting up markets to harness that collective wisdom has been highly time consuming and costly. With the advent of supporting technologies like blockchain, it's now possible to set up a prediction market quickly and easily for almost any topic of interest. In essence, this type of market-building tech lets an Investor collaborate with a huge number of entities at once and turn that collaboration into productive insight—by making collaborators compete with one another to offer the most valid insights (e.g., accurate predictions). Some examples of advanced prediction-market platforms are PredictIt, Augur, Gnosis, and Stox. Most of these (and others like them) are powered by blockchain technology, which is potentially transformative for Investors in its own right. As some readers may not wish to dive into the details of blockchain, we cover it (at a somewhat high level) in the Appendix.

Productivity Applications

The fourth class of tools to speed Investors along the path to technologizing involves productivity. All solutions in this class are designed to help Investors (and others) more efficiently use their time. At an abstract level, these productivity applications can be split into two groups: (1) process-automation utilities (sometimes called tools for *robotic process automation*), and (2) search tools. We'll cover tools from both groups at length in later chapters, but we'll give a few examples here.

Smart assistants and chatbots are highly entertaining examples of process automation that we predict Investors will use more extensively in the near future—just think about how much time is spent in (error-prone) typing. A more game-changing example, however, will be reconfigurable *triggers*: microprograms that can take prespecified actions in response to some initiating event. Current platforms to construct such microprograms as "if-then" recipes include IFTTT (which stands for "if this, then that").[16] As we'll discuss later, these automation tools can provide huge boosts to how innovative Investors can be, as they free up resources that can be diverted to more creative, value-constructing activities.

Meanwhile, more productive search capabilities could revolutionize how Investors operate, especially in terms of more effectively leveraging their internal data, information, and knowledge. Relatedly, being able to more precisely and exhaustively search for new investment opportunities could allow Investors to more productively distribute their efforts in portfolio construction and asset sourcing. Additionally, enhanced search could facilitate innovation by allowing Investors to more easily synthesize new data, information, and knowledge from what already exists in their organizations (i.e., more easily find and recombine bodies of data, information, and knowledge). There's a whole host of technologies that can underpin such next-generation search functionalities, and we'll be looking at many of them in chapters to come. Suffice it to say, search is likely to be a mighty, and mighty common, superpower among technologized Investors in the very near future.

(Super)Power and Responsibility

The classes of technologies we've touched on promise to transform how Investors do business—so long as they're used responsibly. Sufficient understanding is part of that responsible use. Here, however, a subtle problem lurks. Many of these technologies, which are intended to tackle complexity, are themselves highly complex. They mask both types of complexity by effectively wrapping them in a black box. The result is convenience: they let users attack otherwise intractable problems with surprising ease. But, as with any superpower, there can be hidden limitations. There are gotchas that can sting uncareful Investors. Namely, it can be hard to detect when some of these technologies malfunction or trace the reason why.

Understanding is the most reliable antidote to gotchas. But there are practical limits to how thoroughly an Investor can understand a given technology, let alone all the technologies it uses across its organization. This doesn't mean that an Investor shouldn't use a technology if it doesn't 100 percent understand how it works at a granular level or exactly where it might bump into trouble. Trading off understanding against efficient adoption is a delicate balancing act that's achieved partly by selecting appropriate tech in the first place. We'll turn to frameworks for making appropriate tech selections in the next chapter.

CHAPTER 4 FRAMEWORKS FOR TECHNOLOGY ANALYSIS

Assessing Superpowers

We've gotten a peek at some of the advanced tools that Investors can leverage in technologizing. Before understanding how those tools can be turned into superpowers, it's important to have one further set of tools: *frameworks* through which Investors can analyze candidate technologies (or even their current ones). The capacity to assess whether a technology is suitable is enormously valuable; even if a particular technology is bleeding edge with ultrapromising functionalities, it can fail to serve its purpose if it doesn't fit with a given Investor's organizational context. Without a proper fit, any advanced technology can rapidly flip from being a light saber to kryptonite.

That said, whenever an Investor does succeed in identifying and implementing an advanced technology that aligns with its unique needs, skills, priorities, and native advantages, the impact can be profound. As we'll see, the best additions of new technology are synergistic. They empower an Investor with new capabilities and opportunities as well as strengthen its existing skills and resources. This invocation of synergies is not just some fanciful, pie-in-the-sky notion taught in strategy courses at business schools (as is the case with many other ideas peddled as *win-win-win* scenarios). Below, we'll touch on the theory behind the genuine validity of these synergies; and in later chapters we'll see empirical evidence on how these tech synergies can materialize in reality.

As far as choosing conceptual models for thinking about advanced technologies, we've already encountered one: our three-dimensional framework for examining the progress of invest-tech, i.e., in terms of inferential depth, data latency, and resource efficiency. This has been useful for studying the trajectory of investment technology's evolution (and indeed, the recent evolution of technology at large in recent decades). Nevertheless, we've reached the point where we'll need to build up some additional frameworks to allow for more concrete analysis on the suitability of various technologies for any given Investor's organizational context.

The Opportunity-Budgetary Framework

The first framework we develop here is meant to expose the interaction between an Investor's technology and its other organizational resources. This *Opportunity-Budgetary Framework* (OB Framework) models two fundamental facets of the organization:

- **Opportunity set**: the collection of investment strategies and investable assets that the organization is able to pursue, given its overall resources

- **Resource budget**: the sum total of the organization's measurable resources, with which it can generate investment returns

Clearly, these two facets are complementary and should be aligned in any efficiently calibrated organization—that is, one whose strategy matches its resource composition.[1] We observe, however, that alignment between opportunity sets and resource budgets for many Investors is something of a moving target. This is due, in part, to the dynamic nature of investment opportunities, as well as the fact that an Investor's target opportunity set may not match the set of opportunities that it can responsibly pursue, given its resources. Similarly, Investors' organizations aren't static systems: they're almost always in flux. Thus, the size and composition of an Investor's resource budget is also continually changing.[2] Any analysis of whether a new technology is fit for an Investor must therefore take account of foreseeable changes to its opportunity set and resource budget—not just their current states.

In analyzing the fitness of any advanced investment technology for its organization, our research findings suggest that an Investor should begin by asking four questions:

1. How would implementing this technology expand our organization's opportunity set?

2. How must the current resource budget change to successfully implement this technology?

3. What positive changes will this technology likely have on the current resource budget?

4. Are the likely net effects on our opportunity set and resource budget close to equivalent?

Answering these questions helps an Investor better understand whether a candidate technology can create positive and affordable impacts on the organization's resources and strategic possibilities.[3]

Organizational Resource Budget

To comprehensively answer these questions, an Investor needs to have clarity on its organizational resource budget, which is composed of its

- operating budget—the money it has to conduct its operations,

- governance budget—resources it has for monitoring and managing its operations (including time, managerial attention, knowledge, and culture),

- risk budget—the amount of risk it can tolerate in its investments and operations, and

- data budget—the capacity it has for managing data to support decision making.

The sufficiency of these four budgets is what determines the set of opportunities the organization can responsibly pursue.[4] Reciprocally, the set of investment opportunities that an Investor intends to pursue determines whether its organizational resource budget is efficiently *balanced* (e.g., that its governance systems are suitable for its allocation of risk, that it has enough high-quality data to support its governance, and that the costs of managing that data fit within its operating budget).

Given that this book is about technology, one might ask why we haven't included a discrete budget for technology—or, for that matter, a strategy budget—as part of the total resource budget. Aren't strategy and technology also valuable resources for Investors?

Well, they most definitely are! But they're special in ways that operations, risk, data, and governance aren't. The most important of these special characteristics of technology and strategy relates to the effects of changing them. A change to any of the operating, risk, data, or governance budgets *might* alter an Investor's opportunity set; although it need not. Likewise, a change to any of these four budgets *might* affect the other three; but it need not do so (it may affect the overall budget's size, but without changing the size or composition of the other three).

Changes to technology and strategy, meanwhile, *necessarily* affect both the Investor's resource budget and opportunity set—by virtue of altering how appropriate these are for the organization, in terms of being *sufficient*, *efficient*, and *aligned*. Tech and strategy are therefore better viewed as elements of an organization that *tie together* its other resources and opportunities. To depict them otherwise in the OB Framework runs the risk of downplaying their special statuses.

That said, despite each having special status as an organizational resource, strategy and technology don't perfectly overlap in the big-picture functions they serve for the organization. Both strategy and technology can help an Investor to identify opportunities and choose between them. Yet they play different roles in determining the composition of the overall resource budget. Strategy is vital in guiding the specific mixture of risk, data, governance, and monetary resources that an Investor uses to generate performance. Meanwhile, technology's distinctive contribution is in helping to convert these resources into one another, or else making them be more complementary.

Substitutions and Synergies

As we've said many times thus far: the main way that technologizing can help Investors is by giving them new capabilities and opportunities, as well as making their existing ones better. Two integral ways tech can accomplish the latter is by letting Investors

- more fluidly and efficiently substitute other organizational resources (money, risk, data, and governance) for one another, and

- synergistically improve combinations of those other resources, for example, in ways that make the affected resources more complementary.

Examining the potential of an advanced technology to facilitate substitutions or deepen synergies among the organization's other resources is instrumental in analyzing its usefulness for any Investor. Probing what substitutions and synergies are enabled is the most insight-generating step of the OB Framework.

In the rest of this book, we'll go through multiple examples of potential ways advanced technologies can enable resource substitutions and synergies for Investors. But, to solidify ideas, we indicate a few possibilities here. For the first, note that "expertise" is generally considered to be one of the resources that fall inside the scope of Investors' governance budgets (Clark and Urwin 2008). In some cases, technology can allow data to substitute for expertise. For example, an Investor might be considering a direct investment into an illiquid asset located in a developing country. Responsible management of that asset will likely require some country-specific expertise, which the Investor may not have (and probably would be costly to acquire from a consultant, especially on an ongoing basis). Instead, the Investor might turn to a predictive data platform to replace that lack of expertise with real-time, data-driven diagnostics on various aspects of risk in that country.[5] In effect, using such technology lets an Investor expand its opportunity set through shuffling around its organizational resources: it frees up (or keeps open) some capacity in the governance budget by using up some of the capacity in the data budget (this new data needs to be managed) and operating budget.

A second example of substitution likewise entails swapping capacity in the data budget for expansions of the risk and operating budgets. It involves eliminating some of the outsourcing of investment capabilities: by choosing to manage more of their own data through using advanced analytical pipelines or database architectures, Investors can run larger segments of their portfolios in-house. In doing so, they can free up space in the operating budget (remember how we said that technology is often less costly than fees paid to external asset managers?) while also increasing their ability to tolerate risk—which can be more transparently controlled when it is dealt with in-house, as opposed to being handled by external asset managers in ways Investors can't observe.[6]

Synergies between organizational resources are even more valuable than substitutions. As a third example, consider how implementing a cutting-edge knowledge management system can create value by making an Investor's resources more complementary overall (we'll deal more with knowledge management in Chapter 8). It clearly increases the organization's knowledge resources (and therefore governance budget), which can increase the overall degree of risk it can tolerate (and therefore its risk budget).[7] And because data is a foundation of knowledge (as we'll discuss next), successful deployment of advanced knowledge-management technology can raise the total organizational value of its own data, as well as help in improving the management of it (both of which implicitly or directly increase the data budget). Finally, to the extent that effective use of such a system could lower operating costs, the organization's operating budget would rise. These are exactly the type of synergistic impacts that Investors should seek in pursuing advanced tech. We think the OB Framework is useful for guiding their thinking in doing so.

We now turn to the introduction of our second framework for analyzing new technology.

The Data-Knowledge Hierarchy Framework

The majority of advanced technologies that we see as valuable for Investors promise to directly or indirectly improve their access to, or quality of, data, information, and knowledge. These three resources are intimately related and form a hierarchy (with data at the bottom):

- **Data** consists of measurements of the world, such as securities prices, temperature, tallies of retweets or likes, words spoken by a political figure, and satellite imagery.

- **Information** amounts to data that resolves some specific—but key—uncertainties about the world, for example, an election's outcome, declaration of war, bankruptcy, or whether some external asset manager earned its fees last year; thus, information concerns events, and can be thought of as *data placed into context*.

- **Knowledge** generalizes information by aggregating instances of it—while an item of information resolves some particular uncertainty, a unit of knowledge identifies ways in which related classes of uncertainties tend to be resolved; phrased differently, information resolves uncertainty in a particular situation, but knowledge is portable across many situations.

Data, information, and knowledge are therefore closely interlinked, and the fact that they form a hierarchy means improvements to them flow upward (and sometimes even downward): technology that could improve information is also likely to improve knowledge; and technology that improves data will probably also improve an Investor's information and knowledge. Hence, this hierarchy can be used to help understand an advanced technology's value in improving inferential resources. Any benefits that are identified at one level of the hierarchy set a lower bound on how valuable that technology could be: the lower in the hierarchy that the benefits occur, the higher that lower bound is, and the more value an Investor can expect that technology to bring to its organization.

There are three essential parts to this data-knowledge hierarchy framework for assessing advanced technologies. The first, as noted, is identifying which (if any) levels of the hierarchy the technology impacts, and how it does so. The second and third considerations are, respectively, the *particular types* of data and knowledge that the candidate technology affects. Information isn't emphasized by the framework because its value is typically more transient than that for data and knowledge.[8] Information is contextualized data that resolves some specific uncertainty about the world: that is, it answers specific questions. Many questions that an Investor may find itself asking are likely to change over time; and the need to repeatedly answer the same question indicates the potential existence of some deeper problem (not just a specific uncertainty) that the Investor should address. Thus, while analyzing the impact of a candidate technology on an Investor's information is beneficial, we think it's far more crucial to carefully assess whether it has identifiable, positive, and material impacts on the organization's data and knowledge. In order to rigorously assess those impacts, it's useful to have clear ways to characterize the types of data and knowledge that exist within the organization (or, equally as important, to characterize the types of data and knowledge that the organization doesn't have, but needs). The rest of this framework focuses on specifying such characterizations.

Characterizing Data

It's useful to remember that data, information, and knowledge don't have any *intrinsic* value for Investors. Their value is *instrumental*. That is, they're not valuable on their own, and can only be sources of value for an Investor to the extent that they enable specific capabilities, or can identify, generate, or otherwise create access to opportunities. Any new data-related technology can thus be analyzed according to whether and how it can affect the degree to which an Investor's data (or some data that it might come to possess) is susceptible to

- rivalry—whereby the possession and use of the same or similar data by other entities diminishes its value for the Investor, or

- excludability—whereby possession of that data by the Investor blocks other entities from obtaining it, or data sufficiently similar to it.

Technology that can help a long-term Investor derive benefits from nonrivalrous data is likely to be of greatest interest, as such technology's value proposition will not crumble if competition for the data that it consumes heats up.[9] Elsewhere, we've described such benefits as "defensible" (see Monk, Prins, and Rook 2019) because they typically tap into an Investor's unique capabilities, or otherwise come from abilities that are hard for others to replicate—and so can create long-term advantages. Contrastingly, benefits that come from rivalrous data are often short lived. As such, technology that has a value proposition based on rivalrous data should give Investors pause. It'll be unlikely to align with their long-term missions, but is likely to steal resources from technology that will do.

While it may not be as desirable as technology that creates value from nonrivalrous data, Investors should also be interested in advanced tech that can give them excludable data—that is, data that can't thereafter be accessed by others. Plainly, excludable data can create private opportunities that aren't available to an Investor's competitors. These exclusive opportunities can be appealing sources of returns.

Excludability and rivalry are useful in quickly diagnosing how a specific new technology may fit an Investor's organizational context. Any candidate technology with a value proposition that relies on rivalrous, nonexcludable data (either as input or output) should raise suspicion. It's more likely than not to be misaligned with the objective of generating long-term advantages.

Rivalry and excludability can be seen as "macro" properties of data that help indicate the prospects of an advanced technology across many organizational contexts. Our framework also takes into consideration the reality that Investors' contexts are diverse, and that how any specific technology impacts a given organization's data will usually be decided by the finer details of its context. Our framework does so by embedding a second filter of data-related properties that takes into account how candidate technologies affect an Investor's data in terms of the following:

- **Reliability**: Is the data accurate, precise, and verifiable (e.g., checkable, error-free, and unbiased)?

- **Granularity**: Is the scale covered by specific, appropriate data points (e.g., continental versus local, or firm-specific versus industry-wide)?

- **Freshness**: What is the age of the data (when was it collected or generated), relative to the phenomena it measures?

- **Comprehensiveness**: What fraction of a given domain does the data cover (e.g., 25 percent of households in Canada, or all new-car sales in Zimbabwe for 2012)?

- **Actionability**: To what degree can meaningful actions or decisions be taken based on the data?

- **Scarcity**: How widely or readily available is the data to other entities (especially competing ones)?[10]

When used to evaluate a given data set, these six dimensions paint a holistic picture of its *relative quality* (which is, for the most part, a main determinant of its value). Technologies that improve one or more of these dimensions for relevant data sets should thereby interest Investors. On the flipside, technologies that positively affect none of these dimensions directly, or few of them indirectly, should make Investors skeptical. They may not be worthwhile uses of resources.

Finally, apart from data properties, this framework for evaluating technology also accounts for data types, of which it distinguishes five: trading data, fundamental data, ecosystem data, model-generated data, and internal operating data. Most new technologies of interest to Investors will have an impact on one or more of these types. The value of that impact will, of course, hinge on the usefulness of that type to an Investor's strategy. Put another way: technology that has little positive impact on the data types that matter most to an Investor is also likely to be of little value to that Investor. We cover each of the aforementioned data types in detail elsewhere (Monk, Nadler, and Rook 2017). We give brief descriptions of them below, however, for the reader's convenience.

— **Trading data** consists of transactional data, such as price and volume records created by buying and selling assets.

— **Fundamental data** entails data that bears directly on assets' fundamental values within specific economic environments.

— **Ecosystem data** is data on entities that facilitate market function or provide services to Investors (e.g., data on fees charged by asset managers, and those managers' portfolio holdings).

— **Model-generated data** covers data that is derived from models (be they mathematical formalizations or mental models).

— **Internal operating data** encompasses all data that are created from an Investor's own operations.

After evaluating the extent to which a new technology may be able to improve its data—by use of the three sets of characterizations above—an Investor should turn to evaluating that technology's foreseeable impact on its organization's knowledge, which is the next segment in our framework.

Knowns and Unknowns

Knowledge is arguably more desirable than data, in terms of being a resource for long-term investing (see Rook and Monk 2018b). But the value of knowledge is in many cases trickier to pin down with much precision. The framework here respects that fact: its approach to evaluating a candidate technology's likely effects on an Investor's knowledge is more heuristic than that for data.

According to Diebold, Doherty, and Herring (2010) there are two dimensions of knowledge that are relevant for any organization. First, there is what is known to it, and what is unknown to it. Second, there is what is knowable by it, and what is unknowable by it. Clearly, for Investors, known and knowable knowledge is preferable to unknown or unknowable knowledge.[11] (Sorry, things get a tad tongue-twisty here . . . and slightly philosophical.) Further, it's of little use for an Investor to realize that something is knowable *in principle* when it has no identifiable way of ever knowing it! Our framework therefore takes a pragmatic stance. Rather than focusing on what is knowable and unknowable, and known and unknown, it classifies knowledge into four mutually exclusive and collectively exhaustive categories:

— **Known knowns (KKs)**: knowledge that an organization is aware that it has

— **Known unknowns (KUs)**: knowledge an organization is aware that it doesn't have

— **Unknown knowns (UKs)**: knowledge an organization isn't (fully) aware that it has

— **Unknown unknowns (UUs)**: knowledge an organization doesn't know it doesn't have

Of these categories, UUs are usually most dangerous for Investors, and UKs are the most wasteful. As Taleb (2007, 2012) makes plain, "Black Swan" events (rare, high-impact occurrences that are not expected) can be hugely damaging in finance, and Investors should wish to make themselves aware of such possibilities whenever feasible—in other words, turn UUs into KUs or KKs). On the other hand, knowledge an Investor has but fails to reasonably distribute across its organization is a poor use of resources. It depresses that knowledge's value and creates missed opportunities by doing so. But determining what is unknown (whether UUs or UKs) is no easy errand, especially when many Investors already struggle to suitably manage their known knowns (Rook and Monk 2018b).

We believe that advanced technology may be able to help significantly in this respect and create durable advantages for Investors in: managing their organization's knowledge; and being aware of its limits. As Taleb (2012) observes, simply being aware of what you *don't know* can often be more helpful for survival than are many of the things you *do know outright*.[12] Still, an ability to manage knowledge is not equally valuable across each of the above four forms. Instead, we submit that the ordering of value is as follows (from most to least value-adding for Investors):

1. Converting UUs to KUs or KKs

2. Managing KUs

3. Converting UKs to KKs

4. Managing KKs

Technologies that improve an Investor's knowledge will also tend to obey this value ranking. In assessing candidate technologies to bring on board the organization, solutions that can positively impact knowledge always merit consideration—but those that achieve tasks nearer the top of this list deserve more of a look than those lower down.

Cost-Benefit Analysis

One framework is conspicuous for its absence in this chapter: cost-benefit analysis (CBA). CBA is a staple of modern decision making in organizations—and rightly so. It helps organizations gain comfort that an opportunity is worth its expense. Yet, the devil is truly in the details for CBA: its standard implementation relies on many fiddly details, like discount rates, assumed operating horizons, accounting treatments (such as amortization and depreciation), and accurate assumptions on the relative sizes of costs and benefits. Apart from trivial situations, calculating values for these variables can be a painful undertaking, especially since there are typically practical limits on how accurately they can be approximated.

Additionally, CBA has a tendency to be falsely reassuring. By whittling down a decision to a single number (or small set of them), there's often temptation to think that basing decisions on such a figure is necessarily "objective" or "scientific." Sadly, such is not usually the case. CBA is, like any form of human judgment: vulnerable to cognitive bias, (internal) political capture and manipulation, and errors in estimation. Such problems compound when the matter to be decided involves vagueness or uncertainties, for example, when it involves an unfamiliar topic, or its benefits and costs materialize over mismatched or long horizons. Decisions about advanced technology fall in this category, because their impacts are oftentimes not fully clear from the onset. They may have unforeseen alternative uses, they may not work as planned, or they might become obsolete sooner than expected. Given such difficulties, we believe that CBA alone is usually not sufficient as a decisional basis for Investors when analyzing technology.

We're by no means claiming here that CBA is worthless as a tool for analyzing advanced technology. Instead, what we're saying is that we've found it to not suffice on its own to give Investors a sound understanding of what a particular technology could do (or not do) for their organizations. We therefore suggest that CBA be used in conjunction with the frameworks we've presented here, along with other, more situation-specific rubrics we'll encounter in chapters ahead.

CHAPTER 5   TEMPLATE FOR A TECHNOLOGIZED INVESTOR

The Archetype

Let's design a tech superhero! We've laid the groundwork by: (1) thoroughly investigating the roots of Investors' tech problems, (2) exploring the general classes of advanced solutions Investors may use in technologizing, and (3) building up a toolkit of analytic frameworks to assess how well those technologies (and any others) fit with an Investor's organizational context. We're now in a position to assemble these pieces into a full model of a technologized institutional-investment organization.

Of course, we must account for the fact that every Investor is different. Each has its own distinct resources, ambitions, restrictions, and history. For this reason, the model we construct here is *archetypal*. It's one we think has the most features that will be shared by all Investors—regardless of the distinguishing details in their own specific situations—yet will still allow them to successfully technologize for the long run. We must, however, balance generality against granularity: we need to construct our archetype with a fine enough grain to give Investors a clear depiction of the target at which they're aiming. This need for balance leads us to a roster of thirteen features that our overall research finds technologized Investors should possess. Each of these features represents a property—either a priority or capability—that an Investor should have if it seeks to reorient its organization around technology.

These thirteen features of a technologized Investor divide into two groups: *Core Attributes* and *Sources of Advantage*. The distinction between these two is subtle but meaningful. Core Attributes can be understood as the most integral characteristics of an Investor's organization that permit it to technologize. They are the necessary features an Investor must have to become a tech superhero (although by themselves they aren't sufficient to do so). Sources of Advantage are features that will most directly help an Investor to build defensible advantages in technology—advantages that are durable and unassailable. Because many of those advantages will differ from one Investor to the next, the features in the Sources of Advantage group are appreciably more focused than Core Attributes (for many Investors, they might also be more readily achievable in the short term).[1] Still, they're all applicable to any Investor, and each lends something distinct to technologizing. Collectively, these thirteen features make up a reliable recipe for helping any Investor to technologize.

The rest of this chapter is dedicated to building our archetype of a technologized Investor, feature by feature. But before launching into that process, we'd like to flag (what we think is) a general point about the prominence of technology in a technologized organization. It might sound strange to hear, but technology in a technologically oriented organization needn't be *conspicuous* to have a material impact. Think about most Apple products. They're packed with sophisticated technology but are (for the most part) so intuitive to use it's easy to forget that. They're built to empower users in ways that feel natural to the user. They do so by making *user experience* their most essential design consideration. This same principle should guide Investors on their path to technologizing. Technology mustn't get in the way of people doing their jobs, be the subject of every meeting and conversation, or soak up most other resources in a technologized organization.

Quite the opposite is true. In a technologized organization, technology helps people to do their jobs better—it doesn't become their jobs. It creates deeper, more efficient interaction between people, without dominating interpersonal exchanges (calls, meetings, etc.). And it doesn't take the place of other organizational assets and resources. Rather, it strengthens them by integrating them.

Hence, technology shouldn't be in the foreground at all times and places within a technologized organization: technologized Investors must always seek to "own" their technology, without being owned by it.

Core Attributes

Our research identifies three Core Attributes that will characterize any successfully technologized Investor. These attributes involve being

- Culture-centric,
- Hyperconscious of costs, and
- Organized to innovate.

These are the most nonnegotiable features that a technologized Investor must exhibit. They are *the* key forces that'll sustain the superpower capabilities we'll be describing over the rest of this book. And, when an Investor doesn't exhibit them, they're the foremost aspects of its organization that need changing if the Investor is to succeed at technologizing *for the long term*.[2]

Culture-Centric

One of the most colorful, *and true*, quotations we've heard over the course of our research is that "culture eats strategy for breakfast."[3] That is, although strategy is often treated as the map of where an organization is going, culture is (almost always) what steers where the organization actually goes. A strategy that doesn't take account of and align with culture (which we define as the system of norms, beliefs, and informal processes that govern everyday behavior in the organization) is predisposed to failure. Strategy that aims to reorient the organization around technology is no exception. A culture not primed for technologizing will be an obstacle for it. Meanwhile, a culture that is suitably positioned can greatly accelerate and sustain the process of technologizing.

Succinctly: culture and technology are mutually determining, with the fate of one being more tied to the other than may initially be expected. One might be tempted to guess that strong technology can stand in for a weak culture, or that robust culture can make up for poor tech. Neither is generally the case.

It's true that in smaller organizations a well-developed culture can sometimes offset technological weakness.[4] But, for all but the tiniest organizations, a cohesive, performant culture becomes very hard to maintain without adequate technology. The communication and collective commitment needed to support such a culture simply become too hard to wrangle. Hence, for the majority of cases, culture needs supporting technology, and technology needs a supportive culture.

Being culture-centric for a technologized Investor, however, amounts to more than merely having a culture that "supports technology." Instead, an Investor that is culture-centric is extremely attuned to its culture, in terms of its history, present state, and trajectory. A technologized Investor that is culture-centric checks that its decisions on technology fit with its culture *before* it considers adjusting its culture to fit new technologies (especially the informal processes that culture entails). This is not to say that a technologized Investor—or one looking to become so—should treat culture as immutable. Instead, a culture-centric Investor recognizes that cultural change is often harder to realize, and more challenging to reverse when done incorrectly, than are tech changes.[5] Yet, because it's so in touch with its culture, any culture-centric Investor readily knows which aspects of its culture will be easiest to change, if such change is needed. A technologized Investor knows exactly how to *use* its culture to its advantage.

And that's meaningful, as culture is simultaneously the most powerful engine for change, and the greatest perpetuator of inertia, in practically every Investor's organization. That's because culture is, more than anything else, the chief coordinating device in institutional-investment organizations. It not only decides which changes actually occur, but also which persist. In the next two chapters, we'll get a clear view of culture's importance in giving Investors tech superpowers, when we dive into how advanced technologies can help Investors improve their data management and governance (together: *data empowerment*). Cutting-edge data empowerment is perhaps *the* best superpower an Investor can seek to possess. But it can turn into a sore disadvantage if it isn't properly aligned with culture.

Hyperconscious of Costs

It's no secret that we're fervent supporters of Investors being attentive to their costs. Awareness of costs has even greater importance for a technologized Investor than an untechnologized one. Being cost-conscious drives the prioritization of efficiency, which in turn can be jet fuel for innovation—and innovation is one of the chief motivations for Investors to technologize! Of course, most Investors already strive for efficiency (many have little latitude to do otherwise, as they are forced to operate under permanent scarcity). Nonetheless, despite emphasizing efficiency, most Investors struggle at being serial innovators. While efficiency may emerge from attempts to innovate, innovation is definitely not a consequence of attempts to be efficient.

Innovation also needs the right balance of resources to succeed. At present, many Investors starve innovation of resources, since they believe they can't afford it. In truth, however, they can. We cannot think of one Investor worldwide that's paying less in fees to external asset managers or other service providers than it's paying for its own technology. That's a shame. The majority of what's spent on fees could instead be invested on technology that could deliver higher net returns over the long run. A technologized Investor is hyperconscious of costs because it understands this perverse math: it sees that the wisdom of *compounding returns* applies to technology, just as it does to investment portfolios.

But a technologized Investor that's hyperconscious of costs isn't blindly profligate when it comes to technology. No, being hyperconscious about costs means scrutinizing all costs to ensure they're justified and aligned with its success. In many cases, where technology is concerned, costs are more likely to be justified than fees paid to external managers, investment consultants, and so forth. However, technologized Investors must be confident that their spending on technology is efficiently done. Otherwise, they'd be stunting their technological superpowers for the long haul—by steering capital away from resources needed to sustain those powers (namely: people, culture, and governance systems). In sum, a technologized Investor is keenly aware of its spending patterns and willing to spend when it's justified, but fiercely unwilling when it's not.

Organized to Innovate

We've noted that many Investors' organizations starve innovation of resources. But starvation doesn't come only from lack of capital. It also stems from not being organized in ways that give *protected space* to innovation. That is, many Investors ask their teams to innovate, but frequently fail to provide them with ample space to do so. And by "space" we don't just mean physical space (although that is helpful). We also mean (1) time allocated for innovating, (2) freedom to experiment and fail in a controlled manner that promotes learning (and have adequate resources to do so), and (3) the ability to learn from and share findings with others. We will have a long, hard look into mechanisms for creating "space to innovate" in Chapter 10. The takeaway for now is that most Investors are not properly organized in ways that provide and protect space to innovate, which amounts to another impediment on their capacity for innovation.

A technologized Investor, however, must be organized so that it can provide this space. If it isn't, then it won't be able to reap the full benefits from its technology and will be unlikely to derive durable advantages from its technology over the long run. This inability would nix the whole purpose of technologizing in the first place! That's why being organized to innovate is a Core Attribute.

Sources of Advantage

Core Attributes—being culture-centric, hyperconscious of costs, and organized to innovate—are all necessary for an Investor to successfully technologize and sustain its tech superpowers over the long haul. But it's the Sources of Advantage that really permit Investors to fully utilize technology to grow distinctive superpowers and enduring advantages. These ten features are, in effect, the photonegatives of the entangling problems we saw earlier. A successfully technologized Investor is therefore

- cohesively structured,
- atomically focused,
- scientific,
- committed,
- entrepreneurial,
- self-critical,
- apportioning,
- proactively aware,
- neighborly,
- magnificent.

Some of these terms might strike readers as peculiar. They're not often applied to Investors and may appear downright out-of-place. Bear with us. Our research shows that each of them has an indispensable part to play in allowing Investors to transform themselves with technology. We'll briefly discuss each one.

Cohesively Structured

As was discovered in Chapter 2, one of the biggest foes of technologizing is a fragmented, siloed organizational structure. This can come from *spatial separation* (e.g., geography, office layout), *coordination segregation* (where conflicting schedules prevent cross-functional interactions), or *cloistered cultures* (wherein communicational and behavioral norms don't promote fluid mingling or exchanges between different parts of the organization). These flaws cause the breakdown of organizational communication along with disruption of interpersonal feedback mechanisms that allow an organization to embrace advanced tech. Unclogged communication channels and smoothly operating feedback mechanisms are crucial for success in adopting advanced tech for a simple reason: advanced tech doesn't always work as expected straight out of the box. The bugs that may need ironing out can be behavioral as well as digital (e.g., people often need time to get used to new ways of doing things). Being able to quickly escalate issues to appropriate team members, as well as share best practices with colleagues, is at the heart of being able to embrace new technology.

Technologized Investors need *cohesive structure* in their organizations. It might be neither feasible nor practical to restructure the organization to get rid of silos and fragmentation. It's often more achievable to equip people with clear understanding on how they should communicate about technology in the organization—whether expressing problems or sharing innovations—and tools to more conveniently do so (we'll be covering the latter in the next several chapters). This is what we mean by a cohesive structure: one where boundaries between different parts of the organization only exist on paper. Enacting cohesion is partly about facilitating communication (through some combination of culture, governance, and technology), but is also about ensuring awareness. People must be fully informed about where in the organization they should direct their concerns or go for help (whether on tech or other matters). And they should also know where to *push* any new ideas or discoveries on how to enhance operational efficiency and performance. A cohesive structure is essential for enabling that.

Atomically Focused

Counterintuitively, succeeding with advanced technology more often comes from thinking small than thinking big. Large-scale projects and sweeping changes may be alluring—*Let's solve all our problems at once!*—but, for a variety of reasons, they generally disappoint. They can be ungainly to launch and keep on track. They have long wind-up periods and are often no less uncertain than are smaller projects, which are typically faster to implement and easier to contain when they go wrong. Technologized Investors therefore prioritize planning and acting *atomically*. They strive to break technological changes into the smallest feasible units: microprojects.[6] (Pilots, minimum viable products, and small-scale experiments can all be types of microprojects.) Atomically focusing on microprojects buys Investors not only more control, but also more maneuverability on how they engage with technology. With microprojects, they can be more adaptive and agile, which has the pleasing result of de-risking technological change.[7] They can also be more experimental, which is a linchpin of serial innovation. Over the long term, an atomic focus leads to bigger technological advantages.

Scientific

Focusing *atomically* goes hand-in-hand with being *scientific* (we're geeks: couldn't avoid the pun). Investors have long struggled to measure how technology, data, and innovation are functioning (or not) within their organizations. Part of that problem originates in the difficulty of measurement at grand scales. It's aggravatingly difficult to find organization-wide metrics for "how technology is doing" or "the state of data." It's far easier to find appropriate variables to monitor at smaller scales. Further, looking for atomic measurements can often shed brighter light on performance indicators that can scale more globally across the organization. But just "tracking performance" is not enough for a technologized Investor—it's like trying to drive by only looking through the rearview mirror.

Technologized Investors take a more proactive stance on measurement and see it as part of a scientific cycle: *hypothesize, test, measure, analyze, rehypothesize.* Grounding measurements in such a cycle facilitates more concrete thinking on not only what is and isn't working in deploying and operating technologies (... or data ... or innovation), but also how to continually improve. This allows more rigorous analysis and projection of costs and benefits as experience with a new solution evolves (therefore facilitating hyperconsciousness on costs, along with maneuverability).

Committed

Technology, data, and innovation are not typically treated as first-class citizens by many Investors. Investors must genuinely *commit* to advanced tech, data, and innovation if they're to succeed in technologizing. It's all too easy to do something without committing to it. A perfect example is delegating responsibility for parts (or all) of an investment portfolio to external asset managers. Practically all Investors do so, but few are 100 percent *committed*. The role of chief fee officer doesn't exist (whose sole responsibility would be monitoring what external managers are paid, and whether those fees are earned). But it should! And, sadly, Investors rarely club together to behave as "activist investors" toward their external managers—that is, force them to create better long-term alignments with Investors' own needs and priorities, as opposed to having terms dictated to them.

Committing to technology entails not just giving it enough resources to operate. It requires building a budget around technology and the people, processes, and oversight mechanisms to let it flourish. It entails giving leadership in charge of technological innovation a permanent seat at the (highest) table. And it entails enshrining emphasis on technology in a core investment belief.[8]

Entrepreneurial

Without consistent innovation, Investors won't succeed in the long term at reorienting around technology. But without advanced technology, their abilities to innovate will be limited. Investors must prioritize innovation (both in technology and across their businesses in general). Our research concludes that the best way to do so is via an *entrepreneurial* stance. Innovation is not an optional luxury for entrepreneurs—it's required for survival. Investors need to treat it the same way, since, in the long term, the same will be true for them. Crucially, some of the best entrepreneurs have an identifiable *process* for innovating. Investors need this very same thing (we'll be discussing it in Chapter 10).

Still, being entrepreneurial encompasses more than merely having a process for innovating. It requires everyone across the organization to take ownership of innovation. Successful start-ups don't split their teams into two and say: "You folks are responsible for innovating, and the rest of you just mechanistically do what you're told . . . and don't you dare question it!" In entrepreneurial organizations, *everyone* owns innovation. And that requires having incentive structures to enforce that: where each member of the team has skin in the game in ways that motivate them to innovate.[9] Getting everyone to own innovation within an institutional investment organization may involve, for example, evaluating individuals' identifiable contributions to innovating as part of their performance evaluations—in specific, looking at the actual changes they implement in their own work, or proposals they make for improving other functions in the organization (we know of one state pension fund in the midwestern US that incorporates contributions to innovation in exactly this way; we'll discuss that in greater detail later on).

Being entrepreneurial also runs parallel to being scientific and atomically focused. At its core, it requires prizing an experimental approach to doing one's job. Any task has embedded in it an opportunity for improvement, and entrepreneurs relish the puzzle of finding and seizing that opportunity. The best of them do this by experimenting with alternatives in an atomic and scientific way. Building in the time, resources, and incentives to do this is the very essence of giving employees space to innovate.

Self-Critical

Data is the fuel on which a technologized Investor runs. It needs to have confidence that this fuel isn't contaminated by impurities—that is, bad data that has errors, is out of date, and isn't in usable form. Being self-critical is key to confidence here. It offers a process for building comfort over time that data in the organization is trustworthy, since it's then continually being questioned, vetted, and monitored. Technology can shoulder some of the burden for this process, but people also have an essential role to play.

A technologized Investor must promote an environment where people are allowed, and in fact encouraged, to challenge the quality of data (in a respectful manner, of course), and not encounter pushback. People should always feel compelled to ask about the provenance of data: where it came from, who's touched it, and what transformations have been performed on it along the way. They should be critical of data they receive, use, and send. Clearly, having to do that *interpersonally* for every data interaction would be crippling for an organization:

people's time would be entirely consumed by it. That's where technology comes in. Tech can assist in vetting data on a continual and fluid basis—automatically auditing data and complementing the critical mindset. In the next chapters we'll get a look at the mechanics of how this can be achieved.

Apportioning

As we saw back in Chapter 2, many Investors encounter difficulty in balancing agility with complexity in their tech capabilities. Striking this balance is surely a hard problem. The evolving nature of technology and the environment in which Investors operate mean that the optimal balance is both tricky to identify and always changing. Investors thus need to *apportion* decision making about technology. Apportioned decision making entails distributing and delegating it according to a well-articulated and centrally visible plan. This is an alternative to both

- fully centralized decision making, which can be better at managing complexity than agility, and

- totally decentralized decision making, which can be nimble but tends to create intolerable complexity at the organizational level.

Sadly, in organizations where tech (and tech projects) are monolithic, the coordinated delegation involved in apportioned decision making about technology won't work. This is yet another reason why atomic focus is so integral: it facilitates delegation and allows functionality and responsibility to be more discretely divided across people and teams. Doing so is the best way to make an organization technologically adaptive, and thereby innovative.

Proactively Aware

A successfully technologized Investor is proactive in seeking awareness about trends in advanced tech. It doesn't solely rely on incumbent tech vendors in the financial-services industry for its insight on where technology is headed (indeed, it's likely to pay them little attention whatsoever). Nor does it simply look to its peers. Instead, a technologized Investor goes to the source: it's deeply in touch with the community of entrepreneurs and start-ups in invest-tech (although it does, of course, also closely monitor what peers are doing).[10] It has a tight network of relationships in that realm, and regularly has conversations with entrepreneurs, academics, and others who are at the forefront of innovation. A technologized Investor isn't just a tourist or spectator in that world. It's a full, card-carrying resident.

Unfortunately, this is a far cry from today's status quo. Back in 2016, we surveyed more than three hundred endowment and foundation managers on where they source their information about new technology developments.[11] None were at that time "proactively looking" at start-ups, in terms of conversing with them to take the pulse of technology trends, breakthroughs, and so on. Nonetheless, 76 percent believed that the next major solutions in invest-tech would come from the start-up community. That strikes us as a serious cognitive disconnect. Subsequently, we conducted focused studies on eight large public pension funds. Likewise, none were proactively looking to start-ups for insight about where invest-tech is headed, and three-quarters of them relied exclusively on large, established vendors to both provide their technology and keep them informed about the latest advances in the tech world.

We'd like to think that this is slowly changing. Since that initial 2016 survey, we've found Investors who are now cultivating relationships in the start-up arena—in order to stay proactively aware of technology's trajectory. But that approach is certainly not pervasive. Many Investors still take a passive approach to keeping up with tech. And many more don't try to keep up at all. Proactive awareness must become the norm—not the exception.

Neighborly

Although it'll be well worth it, technologizing will be an effortful path for Investors. It's one that will be made far easier by having travel companions. But cooperation and collectivity are rare among Investors. That carries a sizable opportunity cost. It's hugely inefficient, and often ineffective, for Investors to separately diligence new technologies, conduct the same or similar experiments, and lobby their partners for change (e.g., external asset managers and existing tech and data vendors). There are enormous gains to be had through pooling resources—from divisions of labor, to exchanging ideas and best practices, to seconding expertise. Most Investors don't compete directly with one another: not cooperating is wasteful!

But successfully technologized Investors aren't simply collaborators, they're *neighborly*. They recognize that they're citizens of the global neighborhood of institutional asset owners, and that being actively involved in that world—by sharing and cooperating on tech—will make it better for all. Being neighborly doesn't stem from charity, but rather self-interest. Chipping in to the collective makes each Investor more empowered individually. This shouldn't have to wait for formal agreements between Investors on every cooperative opportunity or be mostly steered by expectations of near-term reciprocity. Investors are all in it for the long haul, which makes constructing an open, participatory neighborhood with their peers one of the most enduring advantages imaginable.

Magnificent

Saying that a technologized Investor should be "magnificent" might seem altogether offbeat. But we think it's the epitome of what any Investor should be. We are inspired by Taleb (2010), who observes: "In Aristotle's *Nicomachean Ethics*, the megalopsychos, which I translate as the magnificent . . . thinks himself worthy of great things and, aware of his own position in life, abides by a certain system of ethics. . . . The weak shows his strength and hides his weaknesses [while] the magnificent exhibits his weaknesses like ornaments" (93–94).

We've seen that Investors tend not to fully understand the latent advantages that they have when it comes to data, including their own internal data. Clearly understanding these subtle advantages can be a source of great strength. But equally important for technologized Investors is to be acutely aware of the weaknesses they may have (not just on data, but all tech) and the extent to which these may be permanent. No Investor is perfectly resourced to use the absolute-most-bleeding-edge technology. Yet that's far less crucial than being hyperaware of their weaknesses and strengths, and being honest in strategizing and communicating about both. This hyperawareness is most valuable in guiding decisions such as buy-or-build, wherein an Investor must choose between buying some off-the-shelf solution that may imperfectly fit (or be costly to adapt to their specific circumstances and use-case) and building a solution themselves from scratch. Optimism about the long-term benefits of technology needs to be counterweighted by honesty on achievable reality. This self-honesty would make Investors magnificent.

Adding Superpowers into the Mix

In the above, we've been concerned with the key characteristics technologized Investors will need to build and sustain abiding tech superpowers. Now let's get a direct gander at those superpowers themselves. Over the next six chapters, we'll look at three broad categories of tech superpowers related to data, risk, and innovation.

CHAPTER 6   DATA EMPOWERMENT

World-Class Data: The Ultimate Superpower

For any Investor, the ultimate superpower is mastery of its data. That's because mastery over data enhances all other capabilities, technological or otherwise. In 1668, Thomas Hobbes, the eminent English philosopher, penned one of the most popular aphorisms of all time, "Scientia potentia est": Knowledge is power. As we saw in Chapter 4, knowledge itself is a higher form of data, which implies that data is *really powerful*. The global business community now backs that assertion with gusto. It's even gone so far as to describe data as "the new oil," "the new soil," the "new nuclear power," and the "new ninja throwing star."[1] (Okay, fine . . . we made the last one up. But you get the point.)

But what do most Investors cite as their top obstacles to making better use of technology? It's their own data management and data governance capabilities. Our research indicates that this problem is widely recognized across the industry. Nearly all Investors we've studied feel they're (1) not using their data as efficiently as they could or would like to do, and (2) unsure that they're maintaining suitable levels of data quality in a cost-effective way. These troubles with data have serious repercussions. Some Investors believe that they sacrifice at least 100 basis points in *gross returns* per year due to problems in managing and governing data. That's mind-rippling. It's costing trillions of dollars in benefits in the long run that could be put toward solving major global problems. Further, many Investors are convinced (as are we) that their struggles with data are causing them to surrender an inordinate amount of capital, independence, and strategic flexibility to third parties.

Alarmingly, the situation doesn't look like it'll improve if the status quo is maintained. There's an increasingly large volume and variety of data that Investors must find ways to manage and govern—creating what one senior practitioner describes as a "worsening data deluge." The emergence and continuing rise of big data (especially alternative data) means Investors are facing the need to identify new ways to handle many novel data types, not just traditional data. They're also having to contend with a ballooning amount of unconventional data that's heterogeneous, unstructured, and arrives from an ever-expanding set of sources in diverse formats. Worse, not being able to deal with these data problems could block an Investor from successfully using powerful analytical technologies, like machine learning. Hence, an Investor's failure to master its data could end the mission to technologize before it even starts.

Thankfully, there's a path out of this quicksand: rapidly evolving best practices in data management and governance, coupled with a bloom of next-generation technologies, can empower Investors to conquer their data. This is significant. Data empowerment should be the centerpiece for any Investor's plan to technologize: reorienting the organization around tech necessarily means reorienting it around data. As an executive at a leading Australian pension fund (and dear buddy of ours) says: "You can't build a world-class investment system if you fail to have world-class data."

Of all the chapters in this book, this one and the next were the trickiest to write. That's because all of the diversity among Investors' individual contexts manifests itself more strongly in how they manage and govern their data than it does for just about any other function. Their individual resources and abilities all require distinct approaches, even with the aid of advanced tech. Each Investor has its own unique path to data mastery. But there are plenty of techniques, tools, and systems Investors can assemble to fit their own particular circumstances. Uncovering those is what this chapter is about.

We'll start by making the case for why Investors should revisit ways in which they think about data. From there, we'll explore the forces that'll influence Investors' interactions with data far into the future. Last, we'll examine the human side of strategies that will help give Investors data superpowers. That'll be the segue into the next chapter, wherein we'll take a tour of some of the advanced technologies that can best complement the people component that we address here.

Rethinking Data

Sometimes, to move forward, it's best to first go back . . . to the fundamentals. This is one of those times. Our many interviews, conversations, surveys, and other interactions with Investors have led us to recognize that there's a need to interrogate some data-related norms that have taken root across the worldwide community of Investors. Rethinking these fundamentals sheds light on how a better course might be charted—one that lets Investors be empowered by their data, not hamstrung by it.

Management and Governance

Let's get this out of the way right off the bat: conceptually separating management and governance of data is problematic, even if it seems pragmatic. It has both internal and external ramifications when it comes to communicating data strategies. Different organizations have their own idiosyncratic definitions for what falls under the respective umbrellas of *data management* and *data governance*. Still, the blanket gist is: data management covers how data resources are structured and controlled in an organization, whereas data governance stipulates responsibilities for looking after that data.[2]

This conceptual partition makes some sense. Why not aim to segregate considerations about infrastructure for handling and storing data from considerations about users' data responsibilities—that is, split apart the tech and people sides of dealing with data? Well, for one thing, it can drive an unintended wedge between end users of data and those who are in charge of building and servicing data infrastructure, which causes obstructed visibility and fractional understanding on both sides. A main frustration of teams in charge of data systems and infrastructure is that users don't comply with data-governance protocols. Our research shows this is partly because users don't understand them and are thus frustrated by not knowing where to find the data they need and tools to work with it. Governance fails in part because users aren't motivated to see the big picture of how the overall ecosystem works and their individual importance in it. For them, data management is mysterious. This holds them back from maintaining the right expectations and being more proactive about data use (and governance).

One (hollow) defense for this is complexity. Data architectures tend to be complicated, and users may be perplexed by them. Many enterprise data models look like Gordian knots! That, however, is part of what needs fixing in the first place.

There's also the legitimate psychological problem of demotivating terminology in data governance, which is largely detached from end users' direct interests:

"Data stewards? Governance councils? Yuck . . . those sound like hard work and a distraction. Shouldn't the data management people be dealing with that? I've got a portfolio to run!"

Apart from the internal rifts that splitting governance and management can create, there's also the confusion it can precipitate in interorganizational communication. The boundaries between data governance and management aren't always crisp, and what's on one side of the fence isn't necessarily consistent from one Investor to the next. That can spell trouble when Investors try to communicate about data best practices with each other, as well as when they work with vendors and consultants.

We propose to buck convention and do away with the distinction. Just fold the two together under the banner of *data empowerment*. That does (at least) three helpful things straightaway. First, it conveys that data governance and management are of equal priority and have the same ultimate aim: empowering the business to make the most of its data. Second, it embeds the implicit question, "If some data set isn't empowering end users, then why, for Pete's sake, are we trying to look after it to begin with?" (Data that Investors are obligated to maintain for reporting purposes gets a free pass here.) Last, it'll be smoother sailing to get people excited for *empowerment* than governance.

And there's another reason why merging management and governance ideas into an integrated view of data empowerment matters: understanding. A priority for any data-empowerment program should be that *everyone in the organization* grasps it at a conversational level: in other words, they know how the *overall system* works from a birds-eye view and their precise role in it. We'll elaborate below.

Data as an Organizational Asset

Over the past couple of years, more Investors have been formally recognizing that data is an organizational asset. We're mighty glad to hear this. It shows several changes are underway. First, it signifies growing Investor willingness to treat data as a resource that merits investment and top-level attention. Second, it shows widening acceptance of the fact that users should be obligated to treat data as property of the organization, and not hoard, neglect, orphan, or otherwise mistreat it.

We endorse the progress this view reflects but urge further headway in two respects. For one, we encourage thinking about data as a valuable *process*, not merely as an asset. This, we believe, more cleanly aligns with how data systems should ideally operate for a technologized Investor. Data isn't just raw ore to be mined for gems, or records to satisfy regulators. Making sense of data is *the* central process of the organization and should be set up to enable understanding and innovation.[3]

In that vein, we fear an organization-level focus is possibly misguiding. Data doesn't serve any organization-level goals. It's valuable to the organization only insofar as it informs decisions by *individual* users— it's people that data empowers, not the organization at large. We've seen plenty of cases where data gets subjugated to the "needs of the organization," at the expense of its usefulness to people. Thinking about data at the atomic level of users, rather than the macro level of the organization, better fits with the fact that what users need from data is always in flux.

Takeaway: cultivate a view of data as a *collective process* and enshrine that view within an investment belief.[4]

Data Standardization

During the past two years of our research, we've noticed that a growing gang of Investors is getting serious about prioritizing information. That is, they're shifting from wanting to concentrate on data management to information management.[5] We think this is superb. It calls into question, however, a default expectation in many programs of data management and governance: that, as a rule, data should be standardized, and left in more native forms only in exceptional cases.[6] But standardizing data generally means removing much of the context around it to make it fit a predefined schema. Without doubt, doing so has some benefits for efficiency, and data consistency across the organization.

Nevertheless, standardization as a default can be inappropriate for an organization aiming to move from data management to information management (or even information empowerment!). Recall that information is data *augmented by context*. Whether and how to retain extensive context alongside data is a question that we find Investors increasingly asking. Below, we'll see how some new technology is enabling just that. But to integrate into a data-empowerment strategy that's looking to prioritize access to information as well as data, these technologies may require a swing away from standardization as a default. Instead, we anticipate that a diminishing fraction of any Investor's data will be standardized, and that the norm will steadily become maintaining context as a first priority and standardizing thereafter only if necessary (rather than the other way around).

Relatedly, a growing amount of data's context will become internally generated—that is, it will be created from how people inside the organization interact with and augment it. This spells the need for another paradigm shift: this time from thinking mainly about data storage and how to specify relations between tables in storage, to data life cycles and how data flows across the organization as it matures. The latter view suggests a need to think carefully about the fact that data may gain fresh (unexpected) uses in different parts of the organization as it accumulates more context. This dynamic would increase the utility of flexibility and sharply decrease the value of standardization.

Public Data First

Historically, Investors' data strategies (i.e., plans for data governance and management) have been geared toward data on publicly listed securities. That's unsurprising, as for decades the majority of most Investors' portfolios were made up of those asset classes (and still are). Now, Investors are steadily upping their participation in private assets, including alternative assets. What's more, we've also noticed a healthy spike in how many Investors are building in-house programs for direct investing in private assets. This compositional change in Investors' portfolios invites a rethink of how they're handling data, as the data requirements for such programs differ (often markedly) from those for public ones.

Specifically (and in agreement with trends we've flagged above), this change motivates a need to support more heterogeneity in data while maintaining flexible amounts of context associated to it.

Binary Choice

Finally, but perhaps most crucially, there's less and less reason to frame design considerations for data programs in binary, either-or ways. Older architectures tended to situate thinking in tradeoffs. Consequently, those in charge of overseeing the organization's data often felt straightjacketed into picking one or the other of

- centralized systems that sacrificed flexibility for more comfort in data quality, or
- federated, decentralized setups that were less restrictive, but flirted with anarchy.[7]

Despite this historically black-or-white framing, no pure version of either approach tends to meet needs in practice. Instead, what seems to work is somewhere in between top-down control and bottom-up flexibility. What's more: new technological opportunities are making it so that Investors don't need to commit to a lone point on the control-flexibility spectrum. They won't necessarily be able to totally optimize both, but they can stop thinking in terms of strict tradeoffs.

Currents of Change

We've already mentioned a few pressures Investors are feeling that are encouraging them to be curious about new approaches to empowerment through data. They realize that they're sacrificing returns, relinquishing too much power to third parties, wanting to prioritize information (and not just data) capabilities, and needing to cope with an expanding volume and variety of data. There are, however, a handful of additional *push* and *pull* factors that will strengthen in coming years, and of which Investors should be aware.

First, beyond transitioning to an emphasis on managing (and governing) information, more and more Investors are also exploring knowledge management.[8] We'll have more to say about that topic in Chapter 8, but, for now, recall our definition for knowledge as distilled or aggregated information. This reveals a new angle on how important context is for data empowerment. If knowledge is ultimately to be synthesized from data, then there's a need for Investors to not only have access to more, richer context attached to data, but also to query it in such a way that contexts can be directly compared (and not just explored in isolation). Planning for such capabilities through upfront design (i.e., with a schema for standardization) would be prohibitively difficult. Hence, a desire for next-generation knowledge management creates even more need for *manageable flexibility* in how data-system architectures can be used, in terms of generating insight.

Another (but related) issue is positioning Investors' data systems for advanced analytics, such as deep-learning inference algorithms. These awesome tools are famously data hungry. Yet their performance in practice is critically dependent on how data is transformed before it's fed to them; in other words, there's plenty of *preprocessing* and *normalization* that can significantly affect their results. Some of these data-prep steps are shared across algorithms; others are algorithm dependent (and the specific algorithm used matters—usually a lot). In summary, extensive and restrictive standardization of the organization's data may in many instances hamper the use of these powerful technologies (even more so if these tools are deployed to analyze the context attached to data, which promises to be perhaps the most valuable use of them for technologized Investors). Again, these add to the case for primacy of flexibility and maintaining context in Investors' data systems.

Deep learning and other advanced analytics aside, toolkits used by the rising generation of data analysts are quickly evolving. Bread-and-butter utilities of the past (Excel, the Windows OS, R) are giving way to new standards (Python, Scala, Jupyter notebooks, a need for containers to run virtual machines and packages, among many others). Moreover, rather than licensed software, the bulk of work being done by modern analysts (especially data scientists) is relying on open-source toolkits. This appears to be accelerating the pace of turnover in analytical tools—something many Investors' current data systems are ill equipped to accommodate. Flexibility has to be prioritized.

Softer Side of Data Empowerment

To respond to these pressures and achieve success in data empowerment, Investors will need a two-pronged strategy. The first prong entails more pervasively and extensively deploying some emerging best practices on the soft side of data, that is, how people in the organization view, interact with, talk about, and take responsibility for data. The second entails integrating a collection of new technologies into their organizations. We'll cover the first now, and the second in the next section.

A message that we've consistently encountered across Investors of all types during our work is that their data problems stem at least as much from cultural and behavioral factors in their organizations as they do from any technological deficiencies. In fact, one survey we conducted with over thirty major public pension funds from across the globe found that users' "data behavior" was universally believed by respondents to be the biggest stumbling block to effective data governance. Clearly, data empowerment will have to be *cyborg*—mixing both human and machine solutions.

For readers' reference and convenience, we've listed below the problematic data behaviors that we've found to be the usual culprits behind Investors' data troubles:

- Too little communication about how data is used in, and moves through, the organization
- Too little communication over whether users' needs are met by available data and tools
- Business units not being sufficiently aware of data resources that are at their disposals
- Teams responsible for building and supporting data systems not getting a seat at the table
- Consistent misunderstandings about definitions and roles in data-governance plans
- Barriers to finding ways for investment teams and data teams to smoothly interact and deliver more value-adding solutions for the former
- Not enough capacity for users to self-service on data-related questions, problems, etc.
- Difficulties in ensuring that all data is actively "owned" by *someone* in the organization, and that the responsibilities of data ownership are clear and owners are easily identified
- Struggles to accommodate diverging uses that different parts of the organization might have for the same data set
- Excessive organizational focus on present data problems, while neglecting future ones

To be sure, these are thorny problems to tackle. But we canvassed the worldwide community of institutional investors to identify which best practices will most likely mitigate them. We then put these under the microscope to see how they can be refined to withstand the coming technological changes Investors will face. This work resulted in a set of guidelines for the people side of data empowerment that has two pillars: *global-local comprehension* and *coordinated entrepreneurship.*

Global-Local Comprehension

On the human side of the equation, any successful design for a data-empowerment strategy should start with two questions:

1. How do we get each person to have a high-level understanding of the overall data system?

2. How do we ensure each person knows their responsibilities to and resources in that system?

Any proposed or existing setup that can't find a way to cleanly answer both needs to be trashed. End of story. We're not saying that every person in the organization needs to understand all the minutiae of the system. They simply should be able to explain, in general terms, how all the major pieces fit together—that is, at a nontechnical, *conversational level* (although some roles must necessarily have a detailed, technical grasp). The aim of enforcing this global understanding is to (1) make users better at self-help, by having sufficient visibility to let them navigate the system to find most of what they need, and (2) let them know how their data activities (especially responsibilities) impact others (this latter purpose will be important for coordinated entrepreneurship; we'll discuss why in the next section).

To facilitate this global comprehension, we suggest that multiple versions of the enterprise data model (the overall map of data systems for the organization) be maintained in pictorial form. These should be made permanently available to all members of the organization and depict several different perspectives of the model. For example, there might be one each for data types, organizational functions (e.g., risk management, investment, compliance), and investment units (e.g., public equities, private debt, alternatives). Access to multiple views will give everyone in the organization a grounded, practical understanding of where data resides and how it flows across the organization. To augment these mappings, we also recommend Investors maintain two tools that are likewise accessible by everybody in the organization:

- **A data dictionary** that contains a thumbnail description of each of the data sets that the organization possesses, who *owns* them, their permitted uses, and how to access them

- **A data-tool inventory** that contains descriptions of all the data-related tools used in the organization, whether (and how) they are officially supported, and how to access them

These tools help to bridge the global structure of data systems with a user's changing local needs. We've noticed a rising number of Investors are setting up (or planning to set up) data dictionaries similar to the description above.[9] From what we've seen, these function best when the permitted uses for the data sets they contain are summarized in a quick-reference way. For example, one Canadian public pension fund (with whom we've worked closely) uses a three-level hierarchy:

- **Unprocessed data** can't be used for official reporting, but can be used for research, prototyping, or ad-hoc analysis.

- **Unit-approved data** meets the requirements placed on it by a specific business unit and can be used for decision making within it, but not organization-wide decisions. This data should be fit for repeated/repeatable decision making and internal reporting.

- **Governed data** can be used for all (or almost all) decisions, as it must pass strict quality assurance and validation processes. It's re-usable across different units and different contexts, and has identical quality guarantees in call cases.

Such streamlined classification schemes for data can help to strongly guide appropriate behavior with data. Conformity with them should be ferociously enforced, with a clear message that *everyone* has to follow them—and that any exceptions that are allowed will be rare, and permissible only with explicit up-front approval.

These classification schemes can help accelerate a shift in mindset—away from debates on flexibility-versus-control in *persistence* of data (i.e., its storage). Instead, focus should go to user-centric questions about flexibility-versus-control over what data can be used for decision making.

Another requirement for the local element of comprehension is that every person in the organization is aware of where to turn when they can't self-answer a data question or problem. Reciprocally, users should understand their local obligations in terms of data. In specific, all data that enters the organization should be owned by a particular person. That person may share some responsibilities with others for maintaining the data set, but that one person is ultimately the contact for any queries or concerns about it (including keeping its entry in the data dictionary up to date). We expect practically every individual in most organizations will have responsibility for at least one data set (C-level execs included!).

Importantly, every individual should understand their specific duties in maintaining each data set under their care, as well as under what circumstances those responsibilities may change (including the addition of new data sets as they enter the organization). In general, we anticipate that the assigned owner of a given data set will usually be the person who uses it most intensively. A data owner's responsibilities will vary according to details of the data set, how and how widely it's used in the organization, and the specific technology the organization uses to store that data set.

At the system level, how responsibilities are determined is of the utmost importance. Our research suggests that self-determination and use patterns should guide allocation of responsibilities. In the first instance, we think that (unless there's an immediate expectation that a new data set will be needed in high-level decision making or for organization-wide use) the initial acquirer of a data set (whether a unit or person) should set requirements for format, quality, updating, and so on.[10] Any one-off requests or need for that data set thereafter by other users should be subject to the expectation that the user will deliver the data set as-is, but will promptly and helpfully respond to questions about it. Repeated requests for a data set by another person or unit will trigger a need to negotiate with the owner (for reformatting, augmentation, etc., as is reasonable), and possibly even prompt transfer of ownership to that party. If brief negotiation can't land on an agreeable solution, resolution of responsibility obligations would be escalated to a purposed committee, which we'll discuss in more detail below.

First, however, we mention one quick point of advice about an owner's responsibility for the content of a data set. We believe it's crucial that the owner maintain at least one contextualized copy of the data set—a *raw* copy of the data that is unchanged from the moment at which it reached the owner's possession, whether from outside the organization or the point at which the owner created it. At a minimum, that copy should have associated to it some metadata about its sources, time of creation, and any annotations that the owner might think helpful (e.g., concerns on accuracy). The owner may (and probably will) also keep a processed copy of that data, but retention of a contextualized version enables reversion to the original and allows other users to more easily trace or reconstruct some elements of is provenance. (In the next chapter, we'll be extensively covering metadata and its value in context preservation.)

Coordinated Entrepreneurship

The success of global-local comprehension in data is tightly coupled with execution of coordinated entrepreneurship in organizational data. A cornerstone in our vision for data empowerment is that any data system (including both human and technological components) prioritizes *experimentation* as well as access. Emphasis on being able to experiment with data—whether it's to test budding investment ideas, explore novel tool sets, or construct new information or knowledge—is a key to enabling innovation. We posit that setting up a data ecosystem rooted in flexible experimentation is integral to the success of any technologized Investor. Promoting an entrepreneurial mentality on management and governance of data is an ideal mechanism for organizations to achieve that goal.

What does an entrepreneurial mentality on data involve? More than anything else, it's about making sure that data owners get rewarded for having *skin in the game* when it comes to upping the organization's data capabilities. At present, the incentives most Investors offer their people in looking after data are overwhelmingly stick, and practically no carrot (and oftentimes essentially neither). To put it differently, the data economy in most Investors' organizations is more communist than capitalist. That must change. Technologized Investors should motivate their people to proactively contribute to bettering the organization's data by treating them like entrepreneurs and rewarding them for sinking in productive efforts. Merely burdening individuals with responsibility for the upkeep of data sets can create perverse incentives that discourage them from finding new ones or not trying to get data sets that they own to be used more widely across the organization (being an evangelist for a data set one owns may require more work if there emerges a need to maintain that data set in ways that conform to other users' needs).

What's fairer and more pragmatic is to build rewards for data innovation and evangelism into people's assessment processes and (ideally) compensation. One such implementation might follow the lines of rewarding people and teams for bringing new data sets *that others subsequently use* into the organization (and owning them thereafter). The same might go for finding workable new ways for other teams to use existing data sets.[11] Motivating data entrepreneurship in the organization could give rise to a healthier and less encumbered supply-demand dynamic for data.

Of course, it seems unreasonable that internal supply-demand conditions should function perfectly on their own. They'll need help. We propose the idea of *data empowerment gatekeepers* (DEGs) for that end. We think DEGs—in the form of either individuals or internal councils—could have a multifunctional role (if properly incentivized, of course). They might arbitrate in cases where data owners and requesters don't agree. They may help vet proposals by would-be owners who are entrepreneurially seeking to launch some new data set in the organization (in this respect, they could provide some steering and gatekeeping on where energy is spent in pursuit of new data sets). Further, they could help: verify that the organization's technological capabilities are able to support candidate data sets; identify new uses for extant data sets; and be a conduit for proposing new, need-driven technology. Finally, they could be in charge of helping individuals set regular goals on data ownership and entrepreneurship, plus review their progress (and potential upside rewards) toward those goals over regular intervals.

Technology has a part to play on this last potential role for DEGs. We're firm believers that any performant data-empowerment system requires meaningful and accurate metrics to operate smoothly. We propose some foreseeably useful metrics below. They include both metrics about entrepreneurship, and system health in general:

- Metrics that monitor the accumulation of, and user contributions to, a data set's context (specifically in the form of adding useful metadata)
- Metrics for tracking compliance and owners' fulfillment of their responsibilities
- Metrics to track how much time users spend consulting the data dictionary or otherwise searching for target data, or escalating data questions and problems
- Metrics to track changes in the use patterns of data sets across the organization (to help reward data entrepreneurs as well as detect potential problems).

Let's now turn to look at the machine side of data empowerment for institutional investors.

CHAPTER 7   EQUIPPING DATA EMPOWERMENT

From People to Tech

In the last chapter, we exposed several features that should be core to any technologized Investor's data-empowerment system (i.e., their joint data-management and data-governance program). Our work with Investors indicates that any such system should be user centric, flexible, context preserving, and process oriented. Properly setting up the people side of such a system can greatly increase its odds of success, but world-class data systems ultimately require the right technologies. There are two types of technologies that data-empowerment systems need: (1) storage and access architectures, and (2) toolkits for transforming data, enhancing it, and extracting insights from it.

Storage and access architectures—which we'll just call *databases* here—have long posed thorny challenges for Investors, including on scalability, searchability, costliness, and flexibility, among plenty of other concerns. We're sad to report that these problems aren't going away soon. The volume and variety of data, as well as analytical uses for it, are simply multiplying too rapidly for any one database design to keep up—*for now*.[1] That's not to say database capabilities have stagnated, which is far from true. They're just being outpaced by the speed of data evolution.

Indeed, improvements to database technology are now surging forward, which is one reason we're reluctant to recommend one architecture over another—it's often hard to tell whether features that distinguish one from the next are really diverging or converging! Another reason is that Investors don't all have the same starting points in database setups. Each one's configuration is unique. That matters because the target at which an Investor should aim depends on the difficulty of its journey to get there. In light of all this, we concentrate in this chapter on novel technologies that Investors can use in working with data—to transform it, enhance it, and extract deeper insights from it. At this chapter's end, we'll look into a few database innovations Investors should monitor.

Empowerment Tools

Our research identifies five sets of tools that help Investor's people empower themselves with data—and so bring their organization nearer to its maximum long-term potential:

- Metadata
- Inference algorithms
- Data-workflow pipelines
- "Beyond spreadsheets"
- Visualization utilities

These tools are integral for several reasons. First, each of these tools is (in theory) implementable for nearly any current database architecture that an Investor may use, albeit with varying degrees of ease and efficacy. Second, the usefulness of these tools (and the size of capability sets they enable) isn't likely to decrease, even if an organization migrates to more advanced database setups. On the contrary, their usefulness should only increase. Third, these tools form the core of any top-notch data-science stack: they facilitate a staggering (and expanding) variety of analytical techniques.[2]

A fourth reason why we highlight these tools is because they reduce the agony in the *buy-versus-build* question that plagues Investors' decisions about new technology (and is especially acute for data technologies). From what we've seen, bought solutions rarely match Investors' needs exactly. Hence, they require either in-house modifications, or else being at peace with suboptimal solutions. Building solutions in-house, meanwhile, can be slow and painful, and isn't guaranteed to yield the hoped-for results in the end. Both approaches can be pricey and subject to cost overruns, both in terms of time and money.

Despite the shortcomings of either alternative, we've noticed many Investors embrace what we call *buy bias*: they build only as a last resort. We don't agree with this as a blanket policy but do admit that it's sensible to consider bought solutions when they exist (if for nothing else than to emulate their best features). Additionally, the value of any bought solution increases whenever it's extensible, i.e., it can be augmented to support capabilities beyond those that it originally had.

The five tools we'll explore are all highly extensible. They're also generally fast and low-hassle to implement. But wait . . . there's more! They're all available as (nearly) ready-to-go solutions (whether purchasable or free and open source), although some can also be built with minimal effort. In short, the buy-versus-build problem for them is more a question of customization than sacrifice.

Metadata

In the 1967 film, *The Graduate*, there's a scene (overquoted—sorry!) in which the protagonist gets some advice from a would-be mentor:[3] "I want to say one word to you. Just one word. . . . Plastics. There's a great future in plastics." We have "one word" for technologizing Investors: *metadata*. It's a tool that can fast-forward data capabilities like none other. Whoa, whoa, whoa—you might be asking yourself: "Isn't metadata just . . . well . . . data about data?" Sure is. Yet its potential goes beyond just accumulating more data about your data. It's *the* tool for contextualizing data. Context is captured as metadata, so that any subsequent additions to metadata enrich that context. And the context that metadata can capture is fundamentally unrestricted. It might encode a data set's source, details about its collection, records of transformations performed on it—you name it!

But to think a bit more concretely about metadata, let's use the NISO categorization scheme (NISO 2017), which separates metadata into three categories:

1. *Descriptive metadata* that's used for finding or understanding data to which it's associated

2. *Structural metadata* that explains how different parts of a data set are related to one another, or even relationships to other data sets

3. *Administrative metadata* that might help direct computers in processing the data to which it's associated, stipulate who owns or can access a data set, or contain instructions for handling a data set (or other data-related directives)

Looking at metadata along these lines gives clues about its potentially empowering uses. Structural metadata, for example, can be enormously helpful in giving users more clarity about complicated data sets, or be used to track the origins of a data set that is a combination of others. Administrative metadata, meanwhile, can be efficient to use with pipelines (which we'll get to soon) or in helping identify who owns the data set, when it was last updated, and its approved uses in the organization.

Administrative metadata could also make a huge contribution to tracking data flows across the organization. For example, when users access a data set (e.g., by downloading or receiving it), that access could be logged as metadata—possibly with a time stamp, or a list of any individuals to whom it was then forwarded, and so forth. Such logs might be made even more enlightening by recording aspects on *how* the associated data set was used (this is part of an approach to analyzing operations that's called *process mining* [Davenport and Spanyi 2019]). For example, if it were used as input to a machine-learning model, then that fact might be recorded as administrative data, or via a reference to the data outputs from the model (as a structural metadata field).[4] There are no hard limits on what is trackable by metadata, apart from an Investor's appetite for either building tools to automatically log metadata and store it, or else setting up processes that induce people to manually log it. As both alternatives hint, having a *metadata policy* can be a prerequisite for success with metadata. We'll dig into key considerations for such policies shortly. Let's first discuss descriptive metadata.

We expect that descriptive metadata will, in general, be the most valuable form of metadata for Investors. For one, it can give both humans and machines additional context to understand the underlying data set in its own right—such as how it was gathered, what the maximum or minimum possible values for any field in the data set are, how exhaustive the data set is, or any other contextual details useful for working with it (including auditing it). Descriptive metadata might include user annotations or, in the case that it's textual or visual data (such as PDF documents or images), *tags* on its content.

Tags and other forms of descriptive metadata are useful not just for understanding the data to which they're attached. They're also often important for finding that data in the first place. Descriptive metadata opens up entirely new ways for organizations to navigate their own data sets, even their so-called dark data that might otherwise be exasperatingly difficult to locate. It can do so because it's able to serve as the basis for a wide variety of search engines that people inside Investors' organizations can use not only to find specific data they're looking for, but also to have related or similar data sets suggested to them (much the way that web engines such as Google now work on the basis of semantic search—i.e., search *intent* rather than just explicitly queried terms). Descriptive metadata gives relevant extra dimensions of searchability to aid such engines, which are becoming increasingly easy to use and speedily deployed. For example, the start-up Alation gives users Google-style simplicity when searching for data within their organizations, and Octopai allows streamlined "metadata discovery" that can be set up in a matter of hours and works even with heavily siloed data-storage architectures.

Still, emergence of tools that make metadata easier to find and work with can't eliminate one fact: an organization has to have metadata to use it. Clearly, capturing and storing metadata is a key part of data empowerment, as it goes a long way in preserving data's context. But it just isn't pragmatic for an Investor to manage and govern all metadata it could possibly generate. We think it's necessary, therefore, that as part of their data-empowerment strategies, Investors pick a stance on how they plan to use their metadata, in the near and distant futures. We've seen some Investors that are hewing to a keep-all-we-feasibly-can philosophy in the hope that much of the metadata they retain will eventually bring in some quantum of value for the business. Others are stingier on what metadata they retain and will commit to managing metadata only after a justifiable use case has been pinpointed.

We don't think it's necessarily better for an Investor to be near one end of this spectrum or the other—at least not right now. The important thing at present is that people in the organization are aware of the value that metadata can hold and how it can enhance their capabilities: it won't impede them and shouldn't overburden Investors' current data systems. Still, in the long term we think it'll be universally true that technologized Investors will benefit from being able to support large volumes and diverse kinds of metadata. To reach that point, Investors must prioritize. They should identify their most useful metadata, support that first, and incrementally expand from there.

Inference Algorithms

Since we've already explained the burgeoning power of inference algorithms for Investors (back in Chapter 3), there's little need to recite their benefits again here. What we will briefly describe, however, is the growing variety of ways Investors can access these tools. For example, they can be accessed (among other ways):

- In-browser, for use on remotely stored (perhaps cloud-stored) data
- Through local applications (i.e., that operate on a user's hard drive and have intuitive, graphical interfaces), for use on locally or remotely stored data
- Callable packages in code scripts (written in, e.g., Python, R, or JavaScript) that work on either local or remote data

This flexibility means these tools are, and will become increasingly, available in ways that balance ease-of-use, customizability, and technical performance. That's a genuine boon for Investors, so long as (1) their people don't become overloaded with choice, and (2) technology staff in charge of those tools aren't bogged down in supporting them. The former can be a real problem when people are using distinct configurations, as they'll find it harder to learn from one another. Also, each of these methods for deploying inference algorithms has its own requirements in terms of ancillary software (e.g., software modules or packages on which it depends) and an unacceptable amount of time can be wasted on tracing problems caused by differently configured setups (trust us— we've been there!).

Fortunately, this is a problem that's readily addressed by existing (and rapidly improving) solutions built for data science and software engineering. Docker containers are a high-profile example. They consist of preconfigured setups (called *images*) that tech teams in an organization preassemble.[5] They "contain" all the components needed to support a particular activity, such as running inference algorithms. Users simply load the relevant image on their computer and presto! (Well, not always presto. But most times presto—if the tech team set it up correctly from the start.)

We've also observed it to be best practice that Investors maintain an internal repository for inference algorithms (especially those that have been calibrated to specific data—that is, trained on that data). These repositories are often referred to as *model zoos* and reflect a philosophy that one Canadian pension dubs "Do it once, then share with many." The intent behind this phrase is that it can often require a lot of effort to build and train an inference model. To amortize this effort, it's best to make it available for others (even if they don't use it as-is, it can still be a time-saving starting point for their own projects). Sharing and communication platforms like GitHub can be helpful to that end (via private, rather than public accounts, of course).

Memory and processing requirements are a final consideration worth noting in the support of advanced inference algorithms. Some simple algorithms (e.g., vanilla regression or clustering techniques) have relatively small memory and processing needs. Others cannot be run on one computer alone and must be spread across multiple units of specialized hardware. Understanding what the memory and processing needs of the organization are likely to be, and its comfort with using cloud-based solutions, is crucial to finding an efficient, performant balance between what hardware it owns and what hardware it pays for as-a-service. (We'll shortly get into more detail on cloud storage and processing, versus owning hardware.[6]) That said, memory and processing constraints can restrict what sorts of analyses an Investor can run on its data, and so limit the insights it can extract. Investors must be mindful of future processing and memory needs when designing and budgeting for data systems.

Data-Workflow Pipelines

Consistent processes are a hallmark of good governance (and pretty much good anything), regardless of whether they involve data. Consistency involves repetition: following the same sequences of steps each time. Some of these steps may not be easy or desirable to automate, especially when they need nuanced human judgment and oversight. Yet skilled judgment is a scarce resource for any organization and should be concentrated on tasks where it efficiently creates value. Clearly, this calls for automating tasks where human involvement isn't absolutely needed. Also, humans tend to make errors more often than machines do on highly repetitive tasks. Investors should always investigate automating such tasks.

Data-related tasks are among the most repetitive steps in any Investor's routine processes. True, some situations call for human creativity and judgment in working with data, which makes those particular activities poorly suited to automation. Far more common, however, are data manipulations that contribute very little value and don't call for creative cogitation. These tasks can include the following:

- Relocation—moving data between files or drives
- Validation—checking data for errors and suspicious values (e.g., outliers)
- Transformation—performing operations to produce new data values (e.g., normalizing data, producing descriptive statistics)

Every data process that mainly consists of any of these three manipulations is ripe for automation.

Pipelines are generally the best tools for automating data tasks. There are a wide variety of them and a broad spectrum of technologies for building them. Pipelines themselves are chains of automated steps (much like recipes for executing data tasks). An example of a pipeline that'll be familiar to many readers is the *macro* functionality in Excel spreadsheets, which lets users record sequences of actions to be repeated later. Macros are handy for manipulating data in spreadsheets. They save time, can decrease errors in calculations and data transformations, and are useful in making calculations more auditable and reproducible. But macros have downsides: they're largely confined to Microsoft productivity applications and can be annoying to debug.[7] Fortunately, there are other pipeline types and tools.

Macros are a chief example of human-activated pipelines: they're geared to work whenever a person initiates them.[8] Another hugely helpful class of pipelines are *triggered*: they launch when some specified event occurs—such as when a new file is uploaded somewhere, a target index crosses some threshold, or nearly any other digitally definable action occurs. Almost all modern computer operating systems have inbuilt schedulers that can execute some single, simple action in response to an event that occurs within that system (e.g., back up files to the cloud whenever some amount of memory use is exceeded). But doing more complicated tasks that are triggered by external events that occur outside the operating system, or executing actions in digital environments beyond the local operating system, can be difficult or impossible to do with inbuilt schedulers alone. Luckily, new tools are emerging that can address both problems.

IFTTT (first mentioned back in Chapter 3) is a sterling example of a highly multifunctional, triggered pipeline. It lets users create and chain together various "conditions" that trigger a specified action, for example: "If the S&P 500 drops by a certain amount, then create a list of the ten stocks with highest trading volumes and email that list to a specific person." Intricate tasks can be accomplished by chaining multiple sets of conditions and triggered actions. What's better, IFTTT enables users to create these recipes (as it calls them) without the need for programming: one can simply use its clean, graphical interface to set them up and manage them (à la drag-and-drop). Two drawbacks of IFTTT are that it's not so good with large-scale data manipulations and works poorly with triggers and actions that aren't web accessible. But there are other triggered pipelines that bypass these difficulties, especially for data sets stored in (or that can be moved to) the cloud.

Another shortcoming of almost all IFTTT-like pipelines is that, while they're great for data relocation, they typically offer only a limited set of data transformations (unless one's willing to undertake some nontrivial programming) and can do relatively little at all in the way of data validation. Other pipelines are needed for transformation and validation. Data transformation is a very important activity for most machine-learning tasks, which require data to take specific forms for inference algorithms to work their magic (in machine-learning practice, transformations are called *preprocessing steps*). This preprocessing can be a time-consuming and error-prone task without pipelines. Further, many of the other stages in applying inference algorithms (e.g., selecting and training them) follow predictable sequences of steps. Employing pipelines for the stages of preprocessing, algorithm selection, and training (or combinations thereof)—along with the additional process of *hyperparameter tuning*—has come to be called *automated machine learning*. A sizable number of services for building pipelines in automated machine learning have appeared in recent years. Prominent examples include H2o.AI's Driverless tool, Salesforce's TransmogrifAI platform, and Google's AutoML. These tools' ascendance is making both basic and advanced machine learning more available, reliable, and efficient than ever.

Still, these tools don't yet offer much in the way of data validation. Nevertheless, machine learning can itself be used as a validation pipeline! A relevant case-example of this for Investors is how a large Investor in East Asia used machine learning to make quality checks on its members' data more efficient. That fund realized that a team of its analysts was spending hundreds of hours in vetting data that had only a modest number of errors in it, and that those errors mostly followed identifiable patterns. That Investor successfully implemented a project to train machine-learning algorithms to spot likely errors in specific data sets. This suspicious data is then flagged for analyst inspection, which frees up the analysts to spend more time reviewing data that is actually problematic and spend less time examining data that's unlikely to contain any errors.

As should be evident, pipelines can be a straightforward and generally inexpensive way for Investors to extract operating alpha (i.e., risk-free efficiency improvements) from their processes.

"Beyond Spreadsheets"

We've already aired some of our frustrations with spreadsheets (in Chapter 1), so we'll focus here mostly on solutions rather than shortcomings. But there's one shortcoming we must highlight that'll help us pin down better solutions. That's the fact that conventional spreadsheets effectively suffer from a *collocation* problem: they store data in the same place that data manipulations are carried out, i.e., in-sheet cells. Going *beyond spreadsheets* will mostly require stronger separation of data and actions on it.

There are many candidate tools that could help Investors move beyond spreadsheets, but we think that two are most promising. We'll refer to these as *notebooks* and *dashboards*. Both of these create more division between the holding or storage of data and analyses performed on it. Fundamentally, this means that both notebooks and dashboards are far less restricted on what they can do than garden-variety spreadsheets are. Notebooks are an especially flexible and broad class of spreadsheet replacements that have gained substantial traction in the data-science community.[9] A key idea behind them is that they function like canvases that access data from elsewhere (often creating a temporary file for accessed data, where it can be manipulated). Users then specify steps for manipulating that data. These steps can be run separately or all together to conduct data analysis, unlike in most spreadsheets (where specification and execution of operations on data usually occur simultaneously). These steps can be written in different coding languages, many of which can be heavily simplified by use of "wrapper functions": the user only has to type in a plain-English command to have the notebook execute a (possibly intricate) sequence of steps. Notebooks are highly extensible and can include rich text (such as user comments) and visualizations. They have become a mainstay in the community of data scientists due to their joint flexibility and simplicity.

Notebooks aren't, however, a universal solution—partly since they start from scratch. Sure, it's feasible to take a notebook that's been used in a comparable analysis and modify it for the problem at hand. But that presumes that a similar notebook exists in the first place and that the person doing the modification has sufficient technical proficiency to alter the starter notebook in the correct ways. The barriers to both are undoubtedly dropping, as starter notebooks for a wide variety of problems (especially in machine learning) are readily available from public repositories (GitHub being the main one).[10] Also, proliferation of *plugins*—which are widgets for automating or streamlining specific tasks—is making execution of complicated analytical tasks in notebooks increasingly easier, more reliable, and less time consuming. That said, much as with spreadsheets, notebooks are not especially adept at being organization-wide documents for coordinated analyses.

Dashboards, however, are organization-wide tools—by design. Notebooks are, in a sense, similar to maps. They're plenty helpful for exploring specific routes and getting a sense of surrounding terrain. But they aren't well suited to provide a fine-grained picture of the organization's performance as it navigates a route. If notebooks are like maps, then dashboards are like cockpits of flight simulators. Dashboards are purpose-built platforms that provide integrated views on some aspect of the organization's status, and how that is likely to change as various possible futures unfold. As with notebooks, dashboards are data-driven tools. But unlike notebooks, they're preconfigured to give deep and ready insight on some specific dimension of the organization—e.g., funded status, costs, gross returns, and many others. An example is the liquidity dashboard built by the start-up Real

Capital Innovation (RCI).[11] RCI's liquidity dashboard lets an Investor upload data on its portfolio and then explore alternate liquidity scenarios—i.e., conduct sophisticated, on-the-fly *what-if* analyses on the distribution of the organization's liquidity. It permits the deep inspection and graphics-oriented interpretation of simulated impacts on portfolio liquidity in ways that would be hard to replicate in a notebook environment (and nearly impossible inside a spreadsheet). Dashboards trade off the flexibility afforded by notebooks for preconfigured richness and comprehensiveness in analytical insight (although we should add that dashboards, such as RCI's, are becoming increasingly extensible). Dashboards and notebooks thus have distinct roles, and both deserve their place within the data toolkit of a technologized Investor.

Visualization Utilities

Much of the human brain is devoted to sight. As a species, it's in our nature to be visual thinkers. It's no surprise, then, that as the complexity of the thinking we need to do increases, the value of a well-designed visual representation does likewise (just go ask your local quantum physicist!). The data and analytical capabilities that we've been discussing in this book aren't well captured by the bar graphs, pie charts, and other simplistic visualizations that've dominated Investors' reports for years. As portholes on organizational performance, they're pretty foggy.

A ballooning number of Investors are seeing the need for advanced visualization tools to understand the rising complexity of the financial and real worlds. We've heard many Investors ask about more performant tools for generating visualizations like hive plots, radial trees, icicle charts, heat maps, geographic overlays, and other sophisticated— even interactive!—graphical depictions. Demand for these utilities will only grow as the power of data tools continues to rise (this is most true for deep learning and other advanced inference algorithms). Luckily, an expanding range of simple-yet-elegant (i.e., no programming required) visualization utilities are available, including tools such as Datawrapper, Infogram, Tableau, and Chartblocks. Many of these already integrate with other data tools (e.g., notebooks and dashboards), which is a trend that will no doubt continue.

The Future of Data Access and Storage

We've shied away from talking much about data access and storage structures for several reasons. First, any comprehensive treatment of the topic would require a lengthy, technical foray that wouldn't fit into one book. Second, the diversity of needs and capabilities across Investors is such that generalizing isn't useful—we couldn't state a small number of configurations and say that a majority of Investors would be well served by adopting one of them. That just wouldn't be true. Instead, we'll close the chapter with a breeze-through of the database-related technologies that we're convinced are most likely to go furthest in meeting Investors' data needs for years ahead.

Cloud

We'd be remiss in not covering cloud-based storage and processing. Whether data storage should be moved to the cloud is one of the most contentious tech topics in the Investor community. The core benefits of using cloud storage are easy to see: flexibility, low effort in upkeep, and the support of third parties (usually big names in technology). Advocates of cloud storage cite its usefulness in being less fettered by legacy architecture, due to the more straightforward ability to reconfigure and add additional storage layers and components. With cloud storage, keeping up with the latest database capabilities simply becomes less onerous, which can really help with data empowerment. But then there's the question of cost. Some claim that cloud solutions are far more economical than owning the equivalent hardware, while others are not so convinced. The truth is, how cost-efficient cloud storage is a function of how skillfully it's used. For the most part, that requires regular monitoring of both costs and use patterns, as well as being alert to changes in the provider's offerings and road map. This is, effectively, the hidden upkeep entailed in storing substantial amounts of organizational data in the cloud: watching out for unexpected cost overruns.

There's also the question of security. Many cloud opponents argue that cloud storage isn't safe and can compromise one's data. The reality behind these claims is complicated and not easily untangled. For sure, moving the organization's data to the cloud can surrender some control. But it's not necessarily the case that doing so makes that data more vulnerable. Remember, few storage systems that are physically owned by an Investor are 100 percent secure. Regardless, it is the case that many Investors are prohibited (per regulatory stipulations) from keeping certain types of data in the cloud. Barring those prohibited cases, however, we think it responsible for Investors to not embrace an anti-cloud stance. Cloud storage might not be the solution for all their data needs, but its benefits deserve consideration, even if that means exploring hybrid cloud/owned configurations.

Cloud storage, however, is only one leg of the problem. As inference algorithms become more prevalent and powerful, Investors' needs for processing power will also ramp up. And unless they wish to restrict their inferential capabilities, they'll almost certainly need to use cloud-based processing power. The cost of outright owning proper hardware to efficiently configure and run advanced algorithms, such as sophisticated deep neural networks, can be substantial. Meanwhile, the cost of cloud-based processing for such purposes is plummeting. And not only are costs of big computing falling: more solutions are appearing that have preloaded setups, so users can run their inference algorithms in cloud environments with very minimal hassle (batteries included!).[12]

If the question were one of processing alone, then we'd be big advocates of Investors using cloud solutions as a first option.[13] That said, processing necessarily (at least in most cases, for now) requires having data moved or copied to the cloud, if only temporarily. For Investors that are unwilling or unable to do so, cloud processing isn't doable. They must settle for either owning specialized hardware or going without advanced algorithms. Neither of those options is palatable in the long run, and Investors who are currently prevented from using cloud solutions should make serious efforts to remove obstacles to their use.

Data Lakes

Data lakes are another divisive topic among Investors. Proponents of this type of database laud the fact that, unlike standard relational databases, data lakes excel at handling large volumes of unstructured data and diverse data sets. Truly, it's been the advent of big and alternative data that's spawned interest in data lakes as a serious storage solution for Investors. Lakes' promise of readily handling metadata and preserving context makes them seem appealing as cornerstones in data-empowerment strategies. Nevertheless, they have earned a mixed reputation for a reason. Without diligent care and attention, they can easily get out of control, which is why they've garnered such pejorative nicknames as *data swamps*, *data icebergs*, and *data graveyards*. We recognize these concerns as legitimate, but counter that data lakes are not by any means inherently bad solutions—whether they're successful comes down to how they're used.

Like any database structure, lakes demand both thoughtful planning and disciplined usage. They can't be allowed to become dumping grounds for any and all data. Investors need a visible and understandable policy on users' responsibilities in adding to or working with data in a lake. One of the more inventive approaches we've heard attempts to cap the data lake's size, i.e., promoting manageability by allowing only a "data pond." Another approach involves treating lakes as data reservoirs: allowing data sets to accumulate there until more formal management and governance can be imposed on them, but regularly purging (i.e., draining) them to prevent excessive buildups. In either instance, it's clear that the people side of a data-empowerment systems has a role to play here.

Despite having detractors, interest among Investors in data lakes is surging. A recent survey we conducted of twenty-one Investors (whom we view as tech leaders) found that over 60 percent were either actively implementing data lakes (5 of the respondent organizations) or seriously planning to do so (8 responding organizations). Respondents that were engaged in data lake projects said that cost and innovation were primary motivations. Data lakes can cost an order of magnitude less than ordinary data warehouses. And their flexibility helps facilitate user experimentation with data. This facilitation of experimentation is increasingly alluring; among the Investors we've studied who aren't yet deploying a full data lake solution, there's booming interest in smaller, data-lake-like components for their architectures. These include *sandboxes* and flexible *staging areas* where data can exist in a less structured or standardized form (if only temporarily so), which allows users to more extensively and freely experiment with it.

Graph Databases

A reality of the data deluge that Investors and others are facing is that, as the volume and diversity of data sources expands, the variety and number of relationships between different bodies of data will grow at an even faster (exponential) rate. Conventional relational databases can't cope with this kind of change. Enter graph databases. Whereas in standard relational databases connections between different types of data must be either manually specified or embedded in complex queries, in a graph database they can be added on-the-fly (in some cases, automatically). In graph databases, relationships are first-class citizens and given the same priority as the data elements that they connect.

We'll have plenty to say about graph databases in the next chapter, as we see their main value for Investors as being a platform for superior knowledge-management capabilities. For now, we want to draw attention to the fact that graph databases are within reach for many Investors. A common belief we've found among most institutional investors is that building a graph database would be either too complicated or expensive for their organization. That's no longer so. A rising number of solutions are appearing (and improving) to help convert components of existing databases into graph databases (either to augment or replace the old databases). Although there are still some advances needed to make graph databases convenient enough for all Investors, they are no longer embryonic solutions. They're fast-maturing and likely game-changing architectures that we believe will be an integral part of data-empowerment systems. Keep a very close eye on them.

From Data to Risk

Database projects can be some of the most costly and arduous tech projects Investors undertake. Assuredly, they can be stupendously empowering when done right. But they're only as beneficial as the tools they enable and the users they help. We believe that one of the most power-packed functions that advanced database architectures can support is risk management, to which we now turn.

CHAPTER 8   REFRAMING RISK MANAGEMENT

Need to Reframe Risk

Q: What should a technologized Investor's risk-management strategy look like?

A: Like a Big Oil company's!

We'll let you climb back into your chair and get your breathing under control before we continue.

That's right: we think that Investors should approach risk similarly to how the oil industry's supermajors do business (sans environmental degradation, displacing indigenous peoples, funding despots, operating as cartels, and occasional bribery, of course). Don't mistake us— we're no fans of the petro-economy. One of us drives an electric car. The other one rides his bike everywhere. Definitely no conflicts of interest here—we promise.

Still, it's hard not to marvel at the efficacy and efficiency with which Big Oil outfits run. And Investors can learn from them, because the two have much in common. Supermajors manage large portfolios of assets with a long-term view (mostly oilfields with lengthy payback periods). They take seriously the need for smart diversification (*selective*, not prescriptive). They're laser-focused on costs but willing to spend at scale when there's a strategic fit. They also prioritize data-driven decisions and constantly seek new forms and sources of data to gain an edge. And they cope with daunting degrees of complexity and ambiguity in competitive, unforgiving settings.

Yet, the most fruitful lessons supermajors can teach Investors come from how the former go about finding, extracting, and managing hydrocarbons. The supermajors intimately understand them at multiple levels (atomic, molecular, geological, etc.) and are truly scientific in how they go about looking for just the right types. And they don't make hand-wavy assumptions on what they're seeking. They do *bottom-up* research to find properties they can use to their advantages. In exploration, they recognize that there are diminishing (typically zero) gains from repeatedly looking for new opportunities in the same places; they realize that the top results come from going where others can't. Then, once they've located a viable source, they excel at precisely extracting only what they want. Finally, they prize flexibility in managing the assets that they commit to and emphasize the benefits from explicitly identifying and factoring in what they *don't* know.[1]

Risk is to finance what hydrocarbons are to the oil industry. Except, much of the investment world runs on risk without understanding enough about it, or how to reliably find the right types of it. As Sir Clive Granger put it, "Risk is a pervasive but subtle concept, widely used and discussed but not well understood" (2010, 31).[2] Ask one hundred Investors "What risks matter?" and you'll get a few thousand answers. That's because risk is multifaceted and contextual. It's also an overloaded term, much the same as *innovation* and *sustainability*.[3] This kind of overloading happens when the complexity of a concept exceeds the fitness of tools for dealing with it. Fortunately for Investors, technologies are emerging that can bridge this complexity-capability gap (not only for risk, but also innovation and sustainability). To use them properly, Investors need to let go of several popular but misguided notions about risk.

In this chapter, we'll help technologizing Investors reframe their thinking on risk. We'll look at how the incumbent financial analysis toolkit fails long-term Investors. To remedy its shortcomings, we propose a replacement view on how to account for risk in the investment process. We then discuss how three building blocks—alternative data, knowledge management, and smart contracting—can be folded into that view of risk to enable technologized risk management. Later, in the next chapter, we'll look at four core risk-management functions for technologized Investors: allocation, benchmarking, flexible access, and cooperativity.[4]

Information Foundation

In the investment community, "risk" has become a catchall designation for many concepts, which are often only loosely related. Here's a short, nonexhaustive list:

- outcome variability
- potential for loss
- complexity
- lack of conviction
- source(s) of randomness

What unifies these descriptions of risk (and most other colloquial con-notations) is the idea that risk implies a *lack of information*. Given enough of the right type of information, and ability to act on it, risk goes away.

Risk's inverse relationship with information is important in light of the links between data, information, and knowledge we noted earlier. It's often possible to convert data or knowledge into information to help deal with risk (or else more fully characterize the absence of informa-tion). As the most basic example possible, think of betting on the outcome of a coin flip. Being told the coin is fair conveys information and reduces the riskiness of the bet (versus knowing nothing at all about the coin). But we might also obtain some information about the coin indirectly: by observing a history of previous flips (data) or apply-ing some general knowledge to the specific coin at hand, for example that typical coins are fair (knowledge) and this one doesn't look atypical.

This convertibility of data and knowledge into information is useful for distinguishing three separate domains that often get conflated:

1. Pure risk

2. (Knightian) uncertainty[5]

3. Ambiguity

Pure-risk domains are situations wherein the absence of some relevant information is fully captured by exogenously given probabilities, and all legitimate outcomes are identified. Fair coins occupy this domain. In the domain of uncertainty, meanwhile, probabilities aren't handed to us; we need to formulate them from data or knowledge. This necessarily leads to less-than-perfect confidence that we'll calculate those probabilities correctly, or even well enough.[6] The domain of ambiguity is trickier still. It's characterized by such a lack of information that someone in it is unable to comfortably state just one number for an outcome's probability. In fact, she might not even be sure her understanding of the situation covers the complete list of all possible outcomes![7]

Decisions in the investment world are definitely not confined to the pure-risk domain. Rather, investment decision makers almost always find themselves in uncertain or ambiguous situations. Yet, most modern financial tools cast all situations in the pure-risk domain, as investors (justifiably) tend to prefer managing risk to managing uncertainty or ambiguity. Plus, it's easier mathematically to deal with risk. For the rest of the book, we'll revert to the convention of using "risk" to describe any situation where there's an absence of relevant information—even when such situations are ambiguous or uncertain. Nonetheless, we ask readers to be aware that many so-called risk tools that are standard in finance become less effective when operating in the domains of ambiguity and uncertainty—sometimes catastrophically so.

Usefulness for Whom?

Interestingly, most of the tools that prop up contemporary financial analysis were born in a period when inadequate technology *forced* acceptance of simplicity. (In fairness, Occam's razor isn't a crazy dictum: all else equal, favor the simplest explanation that accounts for observable reality. That said, if simple explanations don't adequately match reality, then parsimony isn't all that useful.[8])

Anyway, in the 1950s and 1960s, most mathematical analysis was restricted to what could be achieved with a slide rule, paper, and pencil (or pen, if one was careful). This partly accounts for why statistics—and fields that used statistics—at that time made extensive use of the Gaussian (also known as the normal or bell-curve) distribution. It's not particularly hard to manipulate, and it can be characterized by just two parameters. This simplicity neatly fit Harry Markowitz's needs when writing his essay "Portfolio Selection" that was published in 1952 by the *Journal of Finance*. The ideas in it have since come to be called *Modern Portfolio Theory* (MPT), and the vast majority of asset pricing, risk management, and portfolio construction decisions today heavily rely upon it.

From a theoretical standpoint, MPT's simplicity is seductive. It posits a set of assumptions, under which an investor can expect to earn an optimal return, given a specified tolerance for the variability of that return (i.e., her risk appetite). Among the required assumptions are (1) that the investor, and all other investors in the market, are given the exact probabilities that investable assets achieve specific returns in the future; and (2) that these probabilities form a Gaussian distribution. This model has formed the basis of, and shared its core assumptions with, many celebrated tools in finance. These are widely used by theorists and practitioners alike and include the Black-Scholes-Merton model for derivative pricing, Sharpe ratio, Value-at-Risk (VaR), and Capital Asset Pricing Model.[9]

These tools remain staples among practitioners today, despite the widespread recognition that their core assumptions are (sometimes drastically) false. Defenders mostly invoke logic along the same lines as George Box's claim, "All models are wrong, but some are useful." And the usefulness of such models can be hard to contest when, collectively, they seemingly imply sensible things, like:

- Diversification is good.

- Lowering an asset's risk should raise its price.

- It's hard to keep an edge in competitive markets.

- Security prices tend to track the value of their underlying assets.[10]

But here's the rub: usefulness *in general* doesn't count for much. The question that really matters is: For *whom* are they useful? Our research points out one answer: *not* long-term Investors.

There are multiple reasons why these tools tend to fail long-term Investors when it comes to responsible risk management. We could write a whole other book on the subject (and may well do). At present, we'll just cherry-pick the most relevant reasons. First, distributions of returns for most assets are not normal (i.e., Gaussian) over long horizons. (Bear in mind: this is true for *most* assets, but not all.) Over longer windows of time, rare events are more common, and these observably occur more frequently than normal distributions reasonably allow (Mandelbrot and Taleb 2010). These rare events are skewed towards being downside ones and can easily wipe out years of positive returns (many Investors are still recovering from the 2008 global financial crisis). And this nonnormality doesn't magically get washed away at aggregate levels, for example, for global public equities.[11] Extensive diversification can't protect against these big downward jumps, but can *increase* exposure to them.

Second, the free lunch promised by full diversification is a partial fiction that really only exists if one can own the entire market portfolio. No one does or can. Many try to wave this off by owning large segments of the market—mostly easy-to-access public securities. Doing so actually makes for an expensive lunch in most cases. There are opportunity costs in not holding some assets and nonzero costs to owning any asset. A portfolio full of a very large number of underperforming assets doesn't provide cheap risk management: it's neither cheap nor effective at managing risk. This is even more true when the assets in the portfolio are also owned by practically everyone else.

Dangerous Starting Point

The process of responsibly constructing any long-term portfolio has two stages: (1) identifying the Investor's unique advantages, and (2) finding ways to capitalize on them by taking corresponding positions in relevant assets.[12] In most views, capitalizing on unique advantages is considered *active investing*.[13] In this sense, we think (successful) long-term investing necessarily entails active investing. Yet, most popular approaches to active investing don't start with identifying unique advantages. They begin by assuming that Investors will hold the market portfolio and then make selective modifications or deviations from it. Yet starting with the market portfolio as a default and then selectively excluding assets is, in our view, dangerous. That may sound like heresy. But it's true.

The "let's-passively-own-everything-and-then-deviate-from-there" approach forces the wrong mindset. It implicitly assumes as a starting point that Investors have no special advantages over anyone else in any market. But we know this assumption of no special advantages is false! At the very least, long-term Investors have on their side the special weapon of *patience*. They can tolerate longer holding periods (and, by virtue of that, more illiquidity) than most other players in the market can. Many Investors also have locational advantages that afford privileged access to opportunities or ideas or have a sponsor that provides some special and excludable knowledge. In short, starting from an assumption that Investors don't have advantages can lead to a very different portfolio than building a portfolio that's designed around advantages in the first place.

Recall how we claimed earlier that Investors' risk-management strategies should emulate how Big Oil companies go about their business. Big Oil's methodology fundamentally consists of

- trying to actively understand the risks they do take (ideally at multiple levels);

- selectively adding risks and assets, rather than selectively excluding them;

- starting from looking for opportunities in places where they have advantages; and

- trying to value information and data they don't have, and what they don't know.

Mirroring this approach to risk management will empower long-term Investors, especially those that take on the adventure of technologizing. Trying to comprehensively justify risks that are taken (rather than accepting the same risks as everyone else and electing to more deeply explore only a few) is a far more responsible way to successfully build—and keep—durable advantages over time.

That's because this approach compels Investors to think about and value what information (and also data and knowledge) they *don't* have. Thinking about risk taking as premised on a need to *understand* risk taps into the inverse relationship between information and risk. If you have more information than someone else, then you can take more risk than they can (all else equal). This is a better way to tackle risk budgeting than assuming some amount of future variability in the prices of assets (which is an inductive exercise that usually just extrapolates the past). Think of risk budgets as allocating the overall *lack of actionable information* that the organization can tolerate.[14] This tolerance is a valuable resource; it should be fully distributed.[15] Risky assets are those that are "expensive" in the budget, as they have a relatively large lack of information.[16] Yet they become less expensive when other market players can't act after that lack of information disappears (i.e., information arrives). The more actionable the information is for a given Investor relative to everyone else, the less of a problem the (temporary) absence of that information is (thus, there's more room in its risk budget). Fully diversified portfolios are thereby doubly expensive. There's a huge amount of information that's missing from them, and most assets in them are no more actionable for Investors than they are for other players.

This view thus engenders a new starting point in risk management that's fit for technologized Investors:

1. Begin by identifying the organization's unique or rare (comparative) advantages.

2. Identify how these advantages can be used to access *processes* that generate meaningful economic value. Then, evaluate the extent to which the organization desires those properties (e.g., in terms of stability, growth rate, cyclicality).

3. Assess how much information the organization lacks on those opportunities and how that compares with information others in the market don't have. Also assess how actionable that information's arrival would be for the organization, relative to how actionable it would be for other players in the market.

4. Determine whether there's room in the risk budget for the opportunity and how rewarding it's likely to be in the long term, compared to other possibilities.

5. Try to find data or knowledge to convert into information about the opportunity.

We're sorry if the preceding seemed a tad rant-y. It's just that we're passionate about these ideas because we care about Investors. A lot. We badly want them to succeed, and paradigms they currently have at their disposal aren't working. Moreover, many people wrongly see pensions or sovereign funds as having disadvantages in the market. It's true that their governance setups can create problems, but it's equally true that they're endowed with some extraordinary advantages. Mixing in advanced technology can go a long way toward unfurling those advantages. But for long-term Investors to really uncork their superpowers, they need some altogether fresh paradigms that complement technologizing. And oftentimes the introduction of novel paradigms is best done forcefully, which is what we've done here. Consider it tough love.

Now, let's look at some tech that can put our fresh risk-management paradigm into action.

Alternative Data

It's easy to see why Investors might believe they have few unique and actionable advantages if the only data sets available to them are conventional investment data, such as prices, trading volumes, and market capitalizations. It'd be insurmountably challenging to make sense of the world if that were your main (or only) window to it. Which is why many market players don't go for sense making: they merely aim to spot transient patterns and beat others to them. Investors have no advantages in playing that game. Alternative data, however, can allow them to play their own game—and win.

We met alternative data (alt-data) a few chapters back, so we needn't reexplain it here.[17] What we'll do instead is delve deeper into how alt-data can be the foundation of risk-management strategies that cater to Investors' strengths. We've observed above how indiscriminate diversification isn't such a strategy: it leaves much on the table by neglecting long-term Investors' advantages, or else relegating them to secondary concerns. Similarly, noticing when others are getting out isn't an approach to risk management that values Investors' strengths. But it's exactly what risk-management strategies rooted in statistical correlations do. The goal of long-term risk management shouldn't be to spot when others are exiting a burning building.[18] It should be to spot the fire in the first place. Alt-data can help Investors notice the flames early, or at least the smoke.

It's worth stating that risk management for technologized Investors has two key activities: identification and action. For long-term Investors, the latter needn't be confined to just reallocating capital. There are more ways for them to act upon changes to information than buying and selling alone. As we'll see, some of the most value-preserving (or even value-adding) actions in managing risk entail interacting directly with an asset, rather than just getting rid of it (in part or whole). Regardless, in responsible risk management, acting on information is predicated on identifying it.

Undoubtedly, it's preferable for long-term Investors to act on information they understand. Sometimes, however, it's also prudent for Investors to act in response to a lack of understanding. In the risk-management framework we've presented, absence of understanding amounts to a big lack of information (and knowledge), which makes any asset to which that lack of understanding is attached very costly in the risk budget—in which case swift remediating action should be taken: namely, exiting the position or directly engaging with the asset (we'll give examples of this shortly).

Here's a parable to help us explain. Imagine you know nothing about tsunamis, and aren't even aware that they can occur. You find yourself walking on a beach. Suddenly, you notice the waterline dramatically receding, which strikes you as strange and possibly a sign of danger. You beat a hasty retreat off the beach and are spared a watery end.[19] Your salvation came not by spotting a titanic wave hurtling toward you, but by noticing a related signal. Alt-data can be a technologized Investor's receding waterline.[20] It can act like Spiderman's sixth sense for danger or Superman's X-ray vision. Having access to alt-data that's linked to activity in the real world can give advanced warnings about risk before they show up in conventional financial data—whether they're tsunami-scale risks, or far less cataclysmic ones.

Let's see a few examples. Investment in infrastructure is an alluring opportunity for many Investors nowadays. If an Investor has a stake in a new-build project at a remote location (say, in a developing nation with poor access to the construction site, physically and communicationally), then they will wish to monitor progress. But poor accessibility will make reports infrequent. Thus, by the time that news of the project falling behind reaches the Investor, it'll likely be even further behind. Delays could create risks of cost overruns, unwanted expenses in additional financing, and so on. Alt-data can help. Companies like Orbital Insight can use shadow-tracking algorithms on satellite imagery to measure the pace of (vertical) progress in infrastructure builds. Monitoring the project with such alt-data can help an Investor more fluidly manage risk—for instance, by knowing when it may need to replace the project manager or phase its injections of capital in smaller increments.

In the above example, the technologized Investor could manage its risk without needing to exit its position in the asset. We'll dig into this idea more fully in the next chapter when we explore *flexible access* as a pillar of risk management for technologized Investors. For now, here's one more related example to whet your appetite. Say an Investor has a direct stake in some food company (could be a producer, seller, or chain restaurant). Aggregating the nutrition and ingredients labels for food offered by that company can help the Investor manage risk in various ways—such as by allowing it to make early estimates of how a commodity shortage might impact costs for specific food items, or how changes in guidance from health organizations on nutrition (or fad diets) could impact demand.[21] Investors could then act on that information by influencing management of the food companies in which it has interests—especially to make sure they're taking long-term views.

Risk management for technologized Investors doesn't only happen midstream. Indeed, as we'll see in the next chapter, it starts during asset selection, when candidate investments are undergoing diligence. Alt-data can help here, too. Consider the task of picking fund managers in venture capital (VC). It's well established that much of any VC manager's skill-based contribution to performance (as opposed to it getting lucky) comes from the strength of its network—its connections to researchers, entrepreneurs, industry experts, and other managers. The value of these networks is mostly treated as an upside measure of potential, but rarely construed as a mechanism to help a manager control its risk. Yet it is—it provides managers with deeper understanding and context about vulnerabilities not only in candidate portfolio companies, but also in the start-up environment more broadly. One way that alt-data can assist Investors here is in providing a rigorous empirical footing for analyzing VC managers' networks. By leveraging data from platforms like LinkedIn, Crunchbase, and Gust, an Investor can gain sharp insights about to whom, and how well, a particular manager is connected.

In the next chapter, we'll be tackling other illustrations of how alt-data can serve the risk-management strategy of a technologized Investor. Let's turn now to how technologies that assist knowledge management can also be invaluable to Investors for more adroitly managing their risk.

Knowledge Management

Managing knowledge intersects heavily with managing understanding—albeit with imperfect overlap. Hence, risk management for long-term Investors *should* depend heavily on knowledge management (KM). Yet our research shows this isn't the case in practice. Most Investors don't have formal or informal KM systems (Rook and Monk 2018b).

Moreover, we've found that Investors are prone to believing several myths about KM:

- Data management and governance must be "solved" before a KM program can be undertaken.

- High-performance KM requires extensively centralizing and standardizing organizational knowledge.

- Top-notch KM is mostly about capturing and transferring knowledge.

In the past, we've argued that these myths hold back Investors' progress on KM. Here, we'll go a step further and state that these fables also hold back more effective risk-management systems.

Underdeveloped KM programs are handicapping Investors' risk-management capabilities because (as we pointed out earlier) knowledge can be converted into situation-specific information, which is at the heart of the risk-management system for long-term Investors that we've described here. A main stumbling block is the assumption that managing knowledge mainly entails managing *what* an Investor knows—what it understands. This is important, but (as we highlight in Rook and Monk 2018b and our earlier tsunami parable) there's also a need for performant KM systems to flag the absence of understanding and knowledge—which can't be comprehensively done by only trying to capture what an Investor knows. What matters more is managing *where* it knows things.

Take, as an example, knowledge about rubles. An Investor might try to codify the fact that holding rubles translates into currency risk that is connected to Russo-American geopolitical tensions and global petroleum reserves (among other things). Knowing this could help an Investor understand situation-specific risk that holding rubles entails (e.g., based upon the state of tensions between the White House and the Kremlin, or the price of a barrel of crude oil). What capturing this knowledge doesn't do, however, is make clear what the Investor *doesn't* know and how problematic that lack of knowledge is. This is where being able to trace knowledge back to its sources becomes crucial: it's imperative to know where in the organization a specific pool of knowledge and understanding resides. Such pools can exist in particular documents or within certain people's minds. Suitably managing knowledge—and with it, risk—means being able to efficiently find these pools.

As we explain elsewhere (Rook and Monk 2018b), locating where knowledge resides in the organization is partly aided by culture, but also enabled by advanced technology. In the last chapter we touched on the transformative potential of graph databases. We see the power of such architectures as coming largely from their ability to support *knowledge graphs*: representations of both how concepts connect to one another, as well as how they link to people and documents. Google's search capabilities are based on a (gigantic and complex) knowledge graph. Knowledge graphs also power Airbnb, Amazon, LinkedIn, and Uber. They're core to the financial search-engine technology of Kensho. And tools for constructing knowledge graphs (on top of or along with graph databases) are increasingly plentiful, sophisticated, and easy to use (e.g., Grakn and TigerGraph). Thus, while they're not yet fully automated, such tools are quickly becoming usable by Investors.

Knowledge graphs are only one (ideal) approach to KM. Extracting knowledge embedded in communications across the organization is another, complementary approach. We've found that effective KM both begins and ends with communication. People can rarely state all that they know (Rook and Monk 2018b), so it's essential to try to infer some of what they know from how they act, and interact, with others. Digital communication channels within the organization—such as Slack and email exchanges—produce an enormous amount of information for every Investor every day. But much of this goes uncaptured and unanalyzed. Tapping this information and synthesizing it into knowledge is today achievable with natural-language processing tools, albeit in relatively simple forms, such as creating phrase-based distillations of mass conversations (e.g., measuring strength of association between "ruble," "USA," and "crude" and turning these into statements cross-indexed to people).[22]

These natural-language tools are also potent when put to uses beyond extracting knowledge from communication. A brilliant example comes from how they're used by NASA. NASA began maintaining a

"Lessons Learned" database many years ago—which contains summaries of various projects, experiments, and test runs. As might be
guessed, some of these cover successes, but the vast majority describe
what was learned from failure. NASA uses natural-language processing
to augment this (enormous) set of records and tease out patterns. These
patterns represent potential new knowledge in the form of interpretable
relationships that might be useful for highlighting what it understands
and what it doesn't (yet) know. Of enormous importance is the fact that
each record in the Lessons database is associated with one or more people, so that NASA can go to the source of potential knowledge to dig in
deeper: to use communication to further explore its knowledge.

The field of KM in institutional investing may be young, but it could
have a dazzling future.

Smart Execution

As we've already observed (and to paraphrase the old-school G.I. Joe
cartoons): *knowing is only half the battle.* Risk management must also
involve action. But many traditional approaches to executing risk-
management actions are not best suited to technologized Investors' objectives: for example, being able to react to external asset managers'
portfolio decisions only well after they have been made (especially in
private equity), or execution of derivatives contracts that are insensitive
to why something occurred. These traditional execution approaches
suffer from too little transparency and reveal too little additional information. That's right: in a well-planned risk-management program, the
actions an Investor takes should be geared toward generating further
valuable information that it can use to guide subsequent decisions. The
reactive execution that characterizes most current risk-management
strategies doesn't do this. It therefore squanders opportunities for
understanding.

A key problem is that reactive execution (such as responding to an
external manager's bad performance) predominantly occurs as nonatomic actions driven by nonatomic information. That is, Investors
often take coarse actions based on aggregated information, such as not

participating in a VC manager's next fund because of poor performance by its previous one, or payment of fees for quarterly outcomes. This latter example is one of the most damaging to Investors' long-term risk-management capabilities. When Investors pay fees for after-the-fact outcomes over relatively long windows of time (e.g., longer than one month), two things happen: (1) they reward external managers only for the *average* risk exposure they manage over those windows, and (2) they miss out on fine-grained information about both risk and those managers' capabilities. Both of these are harmful, but the former is particularly so. It can mask how risky a manager's choices actually were (in terms of their extremes) and so can misrepresent how risky any future involvement with the same manager will be. The latter is problematic because it contributes nothing to parsing luck from skill.

Technologies such as blockchain-based smart contracts offer possible remedies for these problems. By paying fees more continually over time, and tying them to more specific, informative components of performance, Investors could gain more control over their actual risk exposures as well as the behavior of external managers. For instance, fees paid to VC managers could be based on their portfolio companies achieving specified milestones. Smart contracts can make monitoring and payment of such fees less effortful for both parties and enable greater transparency by making criteria for payment more explicit. We'll discuss smart-execution concepts more fully in the next chapter when we cover benchmarking.

CHAPTER 9 TECHNOLOGIZED RISK EXPOSURE

Avoiding Traps

Superheroes are forever lovable, but there's something about them that's unendingly aggravating: their penchant for falling into traps. Sure, taking risks is just part of the gig for any superhero—much as it is for any Investor. But there's a difference between braving danger and being lured into unfair fights with arch-nemeses. Rather than using their superpowers to battle their way out of traps, why don't superheroes try harder at using their special abilities to avoid traps altogether? Yes, yes . . . we know that'd sell less tickets at the box office, but it's rough watching them repeatedly fall for it!

Of course, there are plenty of situations where superheroes aren't cluelessly blundering into a trap: they're well aware of what they're walking into, but their heroism kicks in and they don't see any other way. We've often witnessed similar scenarios with Investors. They exist in a system that's rigged against them—with traps. No, we're not being melodramatic in calling them "traps." There are a few defining features for any trap: (1) it's easier to get into than to get out of; (2) there's a lure, or some camouflage that makes downsides seem less bad or altogether nonexistent; and (3) there are one or more mechanisms meant to put the victim at a disadvantage. Is it any coincidence that many fee structures and LP-GP arrangements seem to tick all those boxes?

We're not naïve. We know Investors aren't oblivious when entering into such agreements. But we also know that in most cases they share superheroes' sentiments and feel they don't really have another choice. Our overarching objective in this chapter is to help in shattering that illusion.

"Hold on," you say. "It makes sense that evading traps is part of 'risk management' for superheroes, yet why so for Investors? For them, isn't sidestepping traps a matter of cost control?" Actually, it's part of a much broader concern: resource preservation. The traps that lie in wait for Investors all turn out to steal resources from them. Money is stolen in the form of unfair fees, while flexibility and control are sapped through lengthy, asymmetric LP-GP contracts (and most other forms of fund subscription). Time is exhausted in the extensive search, diligence, and selection efforts that go into picking external managers. More time and money get torched in paying consultants for benchmarking managers' performance. Opaque, underinformative reporting prevents much-needed transparency. And marketing messages steal confidence (à la "You're not equipped to handle the intricacies of markets. But *our* systems can! Now, be a good Investor and sit yourself down over there. Thaaat's it. . . .").

These are all traps that waste and pilfer resources that could otherwise go to risk management. Skirting traps has everything to do with managing risk. And there's another resource for risk management that the present system steals from Investors that's more valuable than any other: *exposure purity.*

Exposure Purity

As we took pains to show in the previous chapter, for Investors, being responsible in how they control risk exposure means

- being selective in the risks they take and deeply understanding those risks,
- focusing their exposure on the risks that they have advantages in managing, and

- making sure selected risk exposures are likely to be sufficiently rewarding.

This ambition for risk exposure fits with any interpretation of prudent-person obligations. Every prudent individual should, all else equal (or even roughly close to equal), strictly prefer risks they understand over those they don't. Nor should they squander advantages. In this vein, the more selective that an Investor is in managing its risk exposure, the more prudently it's behaving.[1] And being selective necessarily means trying to prevent unintended exposures. There's a need to seek *exposure purity*.

But today's intermediated financial ecosystem isn't set up to deliver exposure purity. While it's true that *factor-based* investing has seen a spike in popularity over recent years (and a sizable number of external managers now pander to this trend), it's noticeably different from the ideas we're describing here. The factors that primarily get targeted in mainstream factor-based investing are vague (purported) drivers of performance—impure abstractions such as "size," "growth," and "value." These are also almost never tied to the specific advantages of Investors who may look for access to them.

One of us has previously explored some concepts related to exposure purity in a research program on "organic finance" (Monk and Sharma 2016). Organic finance seeks to remove distance between the characteristics of assets in which Investors would *like to invest* and characteristics of financial products in which they *actually invest*. Arguments for organic finance parallel those for organic food, which encourage consumers to reduce separation between food as it is when it leaves the farm and food as it is when it reaches the table. The chief lessons of organic finance are to be aware of and wary about "additives" introduced by the productization process. We see organic finance as the first step toward exposure purity.[2] Still, what we're suggesting here goes another turn further. It's not just about an Investor minimizing the empty calories, artificial preservatives, and unknown ingredients in its shopping cart: it's knowing what balanced nutrition looks like in the first place.

If you were to go shopping at an organic supermarket (or better still, local farmer's market), how would you fill your reusable grocery bags? You almost certainly wouldn't purchase a little of everything—nor do so in proportion to how much shelf space each item takes up. But . . . that's what approaches to investing that allocate space in the portfolio according to market capitalizations do. Nor would you be likely to enter the market with an aim of purchasing a fixed amount of food from each aisle. But . . . that's what starting portfolio construction from an asset-class-based allocation scheme does. No, you'd fill your eco-conscious bags according to what fulfills your personal dietary objectives.

That instantly raises the question of what those objectives are in the first place. Most of us recognize that nutritional needs vary from person to person—depending on what that nutrition is going to fuel. An Olympic weightlifter needs a different diet than someone who's just trying to squeeze into a trendy pair of skinny jeans.[3] The one-size-fits-all diets marketed to Investors are traps. They're easy to follow, but unlikely to match any particular Investor's dietary requirements.

There are curious parallels between many fad diets and popular ways for Investors to gain "exposure" through third-party vehicles. You've likely already guessed one: they're geared toward the short term. Picking the right one can give decent results in thirty days but will be malnourishing over the long term (and sometimes fatally so). Many of these also concentrate on excluding specific foods, e.g., carbs, sugars, or cooked meat; they're defined more by what one can't consume than what one can. Then again, most diets that start with what you should eat rather than shouldn't are oriented toward the short run. Just think of the Paleo diet. Sure, it stresses natural ingredients that haven't been tainted by modernity's unhealthiness. But how many cavemen lived to one hundred?

To us, the best inspiration for how long-term Investors should design their risk exposures comes from the nutritional habits of the people with the world's longest lifespans. Health experts are continually making astonishing finds from studying people in so-called *blue zones*: places in which people's average life expectancies are astonishingly long.[4] Members of communities in areas such as Sardinia in Italy, Icaria in Greece, and Okinawa in Japan usually live well past ninety or one hundred. Not only that, they have lower rates of heart disease, cancer, and mental illness than pretty much anywhere on Earth. Longevity researchers trace this amazing healthiness to multiple factors: daily routines that involve near-constant, gentle movement (gardening, shepherding, walking); close ties to family and neighbors; and general lack of stress. But there's one thing that seems to contribute more than any other: what they eat. Practically everything folks in blue zones eat is organic. They absolutely *know what they eat*. Perhaps more importantly, however, they also *eat what they know*. Their diets are almost exclusively made up of food they (or people they live with or next to) grew, caught, or picked themselves. Moreover, those diets embody simplicity. Dishes are uncomplicated and often involve only one or two well understood, fresh, locally sourced ingredients. Total purity.

Technology can help Investors create this purity in managing risk exposure and building portfolios around it. The rest of this chapter is devoted to providing examples on how this can be achieved. We'll look at how advanced technology can help Investors allocate and benchmark risk exposure in more selective ways, get flexible access to purer exposures, and cooperate with other Investors to build exposure when it can't otherwise be found. Throughout, we'll focus on a golden lesson that blue zones have to teach. If you can't find the purity you want or grow it yourself, then don't settle for impurity. Go back to the drawing board and come up with exposures for which purity is attainable, that involve things you understand, and that can sustain you for the long haul.

Allocation

Asset allocation is likely the hardest, yet most important, risk-management activity that Investors undertake. It's also the one riddled with the most traps. For many Investors, it's a two-step process. First, there's some high-level decision on distributing capital, e.g., what fraction to invest in each asset class.[5] Then, there is the asset-selection phase, wherein individual holdings are chosen.[6]

As far as exposure purity goes, this is all wrong—even when the first step involves using high-level distribution rules that *aren't* mere divisions across asset classes. It's wrong by virtue of being a two-step process. The first step essentially specifies a set of performance-drivers, and so reduces the second step to finding investment opportunities that capture those drivers as purely as possible.[7] But what happens when pure exposure to those drivers can't be found? If we're not allowed to revisit the first step, then the only choice is to find the least-bad impure opportunities that fit the bill. Obviously, that's undesirable. Nevertheless, from what we observe, many Investors don't iterate between the first and second steps. Often, the first step is undertaken by the board or senior management, and the second gets delegated to others. Two steps: no more.

The two-step allocation process is also flawed because it typically starts in the wrong place. As noted in the previous chapter, investing should begin with *advantage identification*: figuring out Investors' unique and durable edges over others. Allocation should begin with this same step. Instead, it frequently starts with impersonalized templates, such as (gag) the market portfolio, some heuristic for divvying up capital across asset classes, or some other rule that utterly ignores context.

Every Investor on the planet either already has unique and durable advantages or is capable of cultivating them. These might involve niche expertise that stems from geography, such as

- Californian endowments that have familiarity with the start-up community,
- Australian superannuation schemes with access to mining knowledge,
- Pensions in Iowa that comprehend agriculture and farmland,
- Greek funds that have visibility on the global shipping industry,
- Pensions in Florida that can easily take the leisure-travel market's pulse,
- Icelandic funds that have access to deep knowledge on oceanic fisheries,

- Pensions in Michigan that are close to biochemical-engineering know-how.

Advantages needn't, however, be based on place. They can stem from rich domain knowledge within an Investor's team. For example, an Australian pension fund for the construction industry may have superior understanding of the infrastructure-development process in the Land Down Under. Or a teachers' pension fund in a high-tech area could have a competitive edge in the fast-growing educational-technology market.

There's also no requirement that advantages exist only in the present. They can just as well be long-run, differentiating capabilities that an Investor is confident it can build in the near future. Indeed, most Investors we know and have studied didn't start from identifying unique advantages when they designed their risk-management systems or portfolios. What's crucial is that Investors be able to eventually shift their risk and investing processes to being oriented around advantages (and the sooner the better).

Recall the starting points for risk management that we spelled out in the last chapter. The next step for any Investor should be searching for ways to use its advantages to access *processes* that generate meaningful, long-term economic value, for example:

- feeding a growing world population
- preparing the workforce for economic transformation (e.g., AI-related jobs)
- providing targeted healthcare in an aging society
- building infrastructure that can tolerate mobility and efficiency changes

Finding ways to invest in these processes as directly and efficiently as possible is what we mean by striving for exposure purity. Some would claim this is thematic investing. We eschew that term since it doesn't really focus on advantages from accessing a *process*.[8] Others may claim that these processes are just other types of *factors*. Well . . . they are. But most of the factors with which the financial-services industry is familiar are little more than strip-mined statistical artifacts. And that brings us to an important point—and a main reason why we insist on distinguishing allocation for exposure purity from mainstream factor investing: allocation isn't complete until an Investor has found not only specific assets that cleanly reflect its target exposures but also ways to invest in them that yield sufficient exposure purity. This usually cannot be done with conventional data.

Standard investment factors are based off of conventional data—things like earnings, price, and trading volume. These are undoubtedly useful data points. But they don't really give Investors any profound understanding on how purely an asset captures the sorts of exposures we mention above. And they certainly don't give Investors any *unique* understanding or insight about the asset.

Alt-data is needed in the allocation process. It's needed to gauge exposure purity.[9] And it's needed for pinpointing those assets in the first place. Sourcing methods for locating investable assets in the current, intermediated system aren't very good at homing in on pure exposures. They're mostly meant for finding investable assets by using conventional properties, e.g., historical returns and price volatility, market capitalizations or fund size, or asset class—nothing helpful for gauging any intrinsically meaningful exposures. Putting out specialized RFPs or hiring consultants to run a search process for desired exposures might be slightly more effective but would also certainly be slower and more expensive.

One solution is to "fix search" by associating richer, natural-language-oriented *context* to investable assets. This amounts to (1) acquiring and using alt-data on investable assets to (2) allow them to be found much the same way web pages are found with engines like Google. Google first locates pages (with crawlers and other programs) and then stores data about them (that consists of what those pages contain directly, plus what Google can infer about them). This data (coupled with data on the searcher herself) is what gets used to serve up results in response to web-search queries.

Search in the allocation process could realistically achieve something similar. Notice that most Investors have troves of investment and diligence memos, pitch decks, circulars, and other materials that promote or explore investable assets. But these tend to be poorly organized and not easily searchable. Imposing a consistent structure upon them is hard, and the fields in them that could be of potential value are continually evolving. Interestingly, both e-commerce and e-content companies have long faced a similar problem and have solved it (to revolutionary effect) through using advanced *internally facing* search engines, i.e., search utilities that can index their enormous volumes of diverse products, digital content, and services in ways that make these searchable by customers. Think about how searches on Amazon now work. Imagine if an Investor could do something like that with all of the opportunities it has ever previously reviewed. That's doable—especially with how speedily indexing-and-search tools from companies like Elastic and Algolia are. They often work darn well straight out of the box, even when files are minimally structured and not centrally stored.

Of course, there's no Investor that's seen every opportunity within the investable universe; amplified internal search can only solve part of the allocation problem. There are, however, some appealing new solutions emerging to help Investors locate and assess opportunities that they've not encountered before (and can do so much more cheaply and quickly than with RFPs or consultants). Take, for instance, The Disruption House. They're a young, tech-driven company that effectively serves as a matching engine between fin-tech companies and potential investors. The Disruption House (TDH) generates profiles on fintech start-ups that would-be investors can search along various dimensions. TDH augments these profiles with various forms of alt-data (it incorporates new fields that are requested by investor-users—on an on-demand basis). We expect to see more matchmaking search models like TDH's in the near future to help Investors.

Finally, there will be occasions where pure exposure simply isn't achievable with existing assets. Investors then face a choice. They can either step back and look for other advantages and processes to serve as the basis of allocation, or they can create opportunities that do fit their needs. *Cooperativity* makes the latter more achievable, and we'll be discussing it at the end of the chapter.

Benchmarking

Arguably, one of the most effective instruments in battling poor dietary habits in much of the First World (and a catalyst for the organic-food movement) is nutritional labeling. Nutrition labels help consumers to not only understand the composition of their food, but also what proportion of their recommended daily intake a food item provides in terms of calories, fat, sugar, protein, and other nutritional categories.[10] Certainly, nutrition labels leave much to be desired. For one, they provide guidance on recommended intake only for a hypothetical adult. In reality, the ideal intake for most people will deviate from those values, depending on their individual lifestyles, health statuses, and personal goals.[11] Second, nutrition labels don't give exact values for the specific food item that'll be eaten: they give an average value for items like it (i.e., the specific pack of M&Ms you bought wasn't tested for nutritional composition). That's not too much of a problem for factory-produced food, which will be uniform anyway . . . from one Twinkie to the next. But the wholesome food we should be eating is likely to be more variable, so that static nutritional labels may only give a very rough estimate of nutrition values.

Despite these shortcomings, nutrition labels are way better than what we have in finance: benchmarks. Benchmarks are like nutrition labels in that they give a sense of how well an asset is faring relative to how well it could or should be doing—i.e., whether it's providing the "recommended intake" an Investor needs. They also provide a rough means for comparing assets that have shared benchmarks (kind of like comparing Snickers and Twix bars). All considered, though, benchmarks are pretty weak when you stack them against nutrition labels. They track only a few dimensions of performance and do almost nothing to reveal the sources of that performance.

Weakly informative benchmarks harm long-term Investors in several ways. First, generic benchmarks (e.g., those pegged to the S&P 500 or FTSE) tell Investors very little about *how* any Investment is or isn't meeting their needs in terms of risk exposure—and show them essentially nothing about exposure purity. Second, low-dimensional benchmarks (e.g., ones that convey only quarterly performance) routinely cause Investors to focus on the wrong ingredients of performance and tend to encourage myopia. Third, but not last, peer-based benchmarks (e.g., those that split performance into quartiles) generally assume too much homogeneity between peers.

Conventional benchmarks also provide almost zilch by way of learning value. That is, they give woefully little insight on *why* any asset out- or underperformed relative to some expectation that its benchmark was meant to capture. Unsurprisingly, conventional benchmarks aren't useful for truly rigorous performance attributions (i.e., parsing skill from luck in observed performance).

Still, Investors and others shell out considerable chunks of money every year to consultants and other organizations that offer (in many cases, largely undifferentiated) benchmarking services. We think that money would be better spent on technology to let Investors build benchmarks that better reflect their needs, e.g., in gauging exposure purities, dissecting performance, and learning.

Alt-data and better inference algorithms can help Investors construct bespoke benchmarks that suit their purposes by giving finer granularity, i.e., indicating how an asset is behaving across multiple relevant dimensions in relation to not just ideal levels, but also the thesis for holding the asset in the first place. You heard us correctly: the investment thesis that an asset is supposed to embody should be enshrined in the benchmark for tracking that asset. The objective here is to *understand* behavior of the asset from the ground-up by tracking variables that contribute to its top-level performance (i.e., net returns).

To illustrate, let's say an Investor takes a direct stake in an airport. It wouldn't want to just look at how profitable that airport is compared to others (even in the same geography). Instead, it should want a benchmark—in fact, a sophisticated model—of features that significantly contribute to that profitability, and how much each feature contributes. Features here might be total passenger throughput, number of departures, how many flights are delayed, and composition of airport stores and eateries, among numerous others. Each of these features can be obtained via alternative data (or proxies thereof); and the contribution of each feature to profitability can be derived via use of inference algorithms.

Even without data on other airports, a valid benchmark could be created from such a model by specifying how much each feature ideally *should* contribute to observed performance and then back-solving for estimates of how well the airport is being run by its management team (i.e., determine how efficiently they are managing features that are under their control, given any features that are outside their control). Data on peer airports could help to empirically ground and calibrate the ideal model. Indeed, inference algorithms may even be useful in finding which airports are peers to begin with.

This more constructive approach to benchmarking would be a welcome addition to tools Investors have in many investment domains, especially where they must (for now) delegate some control to external managers. Private equity—specifically venture capital—is one area where more granular, bottom-up benchmarking is sorely needed. Simply looking at the quarterly performance of VC managers' funds gives ambiguous indication on the exposures Investors really face as LPs. Using alternative data sources and inference tools to decompose performance into (1) contributions from portfolio companies and (2) VC managers' timing in calling and distributing capital would be, we believe, a hugely valuable project for the industry—and one that's currently feasible to do!

Flexible Access

The approaches we've described to allocation and benchmarking can greatly help technologized Investors to rigorously monitor exposure purity, along with other aspects of risk and performance. But the value in monitoring exposure and other attributes is fundamentally limited if it cannot be followed by productive action. Being able to trim the sails in controlling exposure is paramount to effective risk management. Yet it's often put into action only through buying and selling decisions.

Technologized Investors can do better—they can achieve flexible access in managing risk exposure. How? Well, let's start by saying something controversial (you must be used to that by now). The securitization and financial engineering bonanza that played a big role in the 2008 global financial crisis was a missed opportunity for long-term investing because it was ahead of its time.

Before sending Ashby a nasty Twitter message, give us a moment to explain. That bonanza was fueled by recognition that the constituent drivers that make up an asset's value are *separable*. For instance, interest payments on a mortgage could be stripped out from principal repayments to be sold as a separate asset—rather than selling the entire mortgage to another party. At its core, this idea of separability provides considerable flexibility to the owner of an asset that has multiple drivers of value. The two main ways this idea went astray (as far as Investors are concerned) are (1) improperly incentivized intermediaries (e.g., big banks) were the ones doing the engineering, and (2) repackaging of the separated value drivers was done in ways that made them highly opaque.

If you remove these two glitches, then what's left? We'd say the possibility for an Investor to gain flexibility in otherwise illiquid opportunities: that is, a chance to fine-tune risk exposure or other properties of returns generation *without* exiting a position in the asset (which can be hard to do for large, not-easily-divisible holdings). This flexible access to selective risk exposure matters:

- It gives Investors some added control over cash flows via interim monetization (and thereby more resources to access other exposures). This can be crucial for exposure purity, in that it can allow investment in assets that may not otherwise have ideal liquidity profiles.

- It can enable Investors to dial exposure up or down as needed. When an Investor doesn't have total control over an asset, then how that asset is managed is likely to change over a long holding period, as is the economic process that asset was supposed to tap. Enabling flexible access through partial monetization allows an Investor to keep its actual exposure purer, while still empowering it with the option value inherent in its ownership of the asset—not to mention savings in transaction costs (which can be substantial for large, illiquid assets).

How can such flexible access (which includes, but isn't limited to, partially monetizing the non-core-value drivers in an asset—e.g., tax credits, royalties, interest) be achieved? Well, usually this'd be accomplished through issuance of some clever derivatives contracts (or else undertaking some form of securitization through an intermediary, which we already know can be problematic). There's a technological solution: smart contracts. Smart contracts can be issued faster than derivatives and, depending on the profile of payments they deliver to the buyer (e.g., timing and scale), can enjoy less of an illiquidity discount—assuming the tokens or other digital currencies in which payments are rendered are popular ones (such as Ether on the Ethereum platform for issuing smart contracts).

With smart contracts, Investors can create the sort of flexibility in real, illiquid assets that once existed (and in some cases, still does) for timberland investments. For us, timberland serves as a hypothetical ideal since it consists of a core underlying asset—land beneath forests—as well as a harvestable, replenishable source of cash flow from that core asset (the sale of timber) that's separable from the core asset: that is, the felled trees can be sold without the land underneath them. Owners of timberland have substantial flexibility in when they can time harvests of timber, along with how extensive those harvests are (that is, what fraction of a forest to log). Moreover, through selective replanting, whether of new or original tree species, a timberland owner can also influence the value of the underlying asset. Finally, timberland offers up many other paths to monetization, such as the sale of carbon credits or biofuel, recreation or mineral rights, and intercropping. These flexible options in managing timberland are something we expect can be replicated in other illiquid assets through the judicious creation and sale of smart contracts. Moreover, there's no restriction (in most instances) on Investors being only sellers of such contracts; they might also productively be buyers.

Cooperativity

We've been harping on and on about Investors creating advantages for themselves. Let's face it: that's hard! As with any hardship, it's also something made better when not faced alone. Indeed, a gigantic advantage that long-term Investors have over other financial entities is their ability to cooperate with one another. Most Investors don't directly compete with one another, whereas most asset managers, custodians, banks, and so on, do. The ability to cooperate with each other to build durable advantages is a superpowerful advantage that Investors have— whether they technologize or not.

Cooperativity can be vital in risk management for an assortment of reasons—namely, it can let Investors create opportunities that fit their desired risk exposures (and so maintain exposure purity), as well as help expand the volume and diversity of alt-data available to them.

As we've pointed out, the exposure purity an Investor may be seeking can sometimes not exist in its available universe of investable assets. The Investor could go back to the drawing board and search for new economic processes (or even advantages) that it may then use to look for new, pure exposures. Alternatively, the Investor could build form-fit opportunities itself: DIY exposure purity. Doing so can be a truly effective way for an Investor to avoid many of the standard traps in finance—it gets complete control and transparency. Nonetheless, building opportunities from scratch (e.g., infrastructure projects or start-ups) can be too resource intensive for one Investor to do solo— and, even if they aren't, there are often unmissable efficiencies that come from partnering with others. Either way, engaging in joint ventures with other Investors can spread risk, pool capital, and allow for beneficial sharing of data, information, and knowledge.

But it's no cakewalk. There are coordination challenges. Different Investors may be chasing different exposures from the asset they're seeking to grow, or, there can be cultural clashes. There can also be concerns that burdens won't be shared evenly, and that free riding can cause one party to gain at the other's expense (which can be an uncomfortable fact to have to report to the board). We regret that we have no perfect solution to the snags here, but we do think technology can play an alleviating role. Many of the challenges to joint ventures we've sketched above are traditionally solved through contracting—either formal or relational.[12] Smart contracting is a third alternative.

Using a series of flexible, small-scale, digital contracts linked to identifiable events (or else the mutual sign-off of contracted parties) can make joint venturing more fluid by

- making objectively measurable contributions more immediately recognized or rewarded (i.e., it helps with score-keeping);
- allowing partnering organizations to more precisely divvy up sources of value in the asset, but possibly change these dynamically when it is mutually agreeable to do so;
- helping partnering Investors coordinate and cooperate despite geographic separation; and
- permitting some parties to partially monetize their positions in the joint asset (for example, if circumstances change significantly) without dropping out.

We believe that other possible ways for smart contracting to help Investors cooperate in building new assets will soon be found. We're deeply excited about the creativity they could help to unlock.

Even when Investors might not cooperate directly by participating in coinvestments, they can still generate immense value by indirect collaboration—namely, in sharing data. Alt-data (and even conventional data) can be expensive to obtain. This cost can come not only in actually getting the data, but also converting it into usable form. Per popular estimates, 80 percent or more of time spent on working with alt-data is on cleaning, checking, and otherwise wrangling it. Less than a quarter is typically spent on actually analyzing it! Imagine the benefits of being able to reduce that 80 percent—by sharing.

We've long predicted that Investors could become heavy hitters in data analytics by sharing data (especially alternative data) with one another, whether through exchanging it or growing it as a collective resource. However, we've been unsure about how much willingness and appetite actually existed among Investors for cooperativity around data. After all, we'd seen no evidence that Investors had historically engaged in any significant sharing of data (except in joint ventures).

We decided to do a study. We put twenty-one large pension and sovereign wealth funds into a room. We asked them to state whether they'd be willing to set up "fair" data-sharing programs with each of the other organizations present (the organizations were each known to one another, but their responses about willingness for data sharing were kept anonymous). We were floored. None was outright unwilling to share data with any other. More importantly, however, almost half (nine) of the organizations in our study were "very likely" to run data sharing programs with at least half of the other organizations in the room. We didn't expect willingness to be so pervasive. Neither did the respondents. In follow-up discussion, participants largely said they were unaware others might be interested in conducting joint data projects. We did this study in May 2018, so we haven't yet seen whether this fresh awareness will foster data collaborations. But we are convinced it should.

Many of the data-management and empowerment tools we've described in earlier chapters can be set up to work across organizational boundaries: there are few technical barriers to sharing data that couldn't be surmounted. Even when it comes to sensitive data, solutions exist that permit organizations to perform analyses on one another's data without direct access to it (a fascinating example is the technology offered by Inpher, which allows organizations to perform complicated machine-learning tasks on each other's data while still maintaining the privacy and integrity of the data: datasets never leave their parent organization's control). Hence, the only real barrier to extensive and productive data cooperativity among Investors is their own unfamiliarity with the idea. It's high time for that barrier to come down so Investors can uncork their joint superpowers.

CHAPTER 10   SPACE TO INNOVATE

Making Innovation Programmatic

We've so far worked to prove the virtues of technologizing and show how any Investor, in its own way, is capable of doing so. We're further convinced (and hope you are, too) that every Investor should do so— apart from in one instance: when an Investor refuses to commit to being innovative.

For Investors, technologizing is fruitless without innovating. To be clear, Investors who are unable to pursue innovation can still make use of some advanced technologies. Nevertheless, any efforts to reorient the organization around technology will fall flat in the long run if the organization can't innovate. Without innovating, the comparative advantages an Investor might hope to generate from technology won't be durable. At some point, its shiny new tech will lapse into legacy architecture: without the momentum that ongoing innovation gives, it'll struggle to make the next hop forward. As one practitioner put it: "There's a need to guard against rocking-horse syndrome. . . . You don't just want technology to come in, create a little movement, but not take the organization forward."

Reciprocally, innovation is blunted without technology. True, Investors can still innovate without technology or technologizing. But they're monstrously disadvantaged in doing so. As this book is about constructing durable advantages for long-term Investors, we'll concentrate on ways Investors can reorient their organizations around both technology and innovation at the same time. Investors that succeed in doing so can use technology to reinforce innovation, and innovation to reinforce their technology capabilities—thus creating a perpetual-motion machine.

For some pioneering Investors, that machine is already in motion, and accelerating rapidly. Encouragingly, over the last two years we've seen a small cadre of about a dozen Investors that are taking bold strides toward making innovation a part of their organizations' central nervous systems. They're thoughtfully, methodically, and enthusiastically, *committing* to innovating. In this chapter we'll be conveying some of their experiences. We'll discuss emerging best practices and explore some techniques and tools that pioneer Investors are deploying to facilitate innovation. And we'll be exploring how Investors are reaching outside their own organizations in the pursuit of innovation partners. In the following chapter, we'll stitch these many pieces together and present an altogether new way for Investors to turn their organizations into innovation juggernauts: *R3D*.

But, before all that, there's one universal truth we've found in our research that's worth pointing out up front. Yes, innovation often relies on a little creativity and serendipity. Those are, however, a very teensy fraction of what makes innovation successful in institutional investing. Instead, success—*repeated* success—boils down to two not-so-secret ingredients: processes and resources.

When processes and resources aren't in place to support innovation, innovation will be sporadic and uncontrolled (at best). Long-term Investors shouldn't be aiming for sporadic innovation (i.e., one-offs that are largely ungoverned, minimally planned, and don't follow any replicable process). That sort of innovation can be useful when it occurs, but it's unreliable and confers little benefit in terms of learning—which is a big part of innovating.

A far more desirable approach is thus to strive for *programmatic innovation*, which is composed of coordinated efforts to innovate that are

- goal-oriented and address real, preidentified business problems;

- equipped with suitable resources that are reserved purposely for innovating (i.e., create protected space to innovate);

- designed to contain and control small-scale failures that result from the innovation process, in ways that yield productive, transferable learning;

- set within a culture that is supportive, engaged, and buys in to innovating;

- engineered to spread benefits of innovation throughout the organization; and

- open to partnering with aligned outside entities when doing so is pragmatic.

The granular details of how any one organization implements programmatic innovation are unique to its own context. Some trial and error should be expected when working to find configurations of processes and resources that work best for a given Investor. Nevertheless, there are plenty of lessons that are portable across organizations—many of which are born from painful experience and hard-won insight. The rest of this chapter is dedicated to passing those on to you, dear reader.

Portable Lessons and Best Practices

Over the past three years, we've had the privilege of cohosting a one-of-a-kind event (with our friends in AustralianSuper and New Zealand Superannuation Fund) at Stanford. It's a gathering of over two dozen of the largest and fastest technologizing long-term Investors on the planet (so far). For three days, attendees share and discuss their organizations' challenges, victories, and ambitions on matters relating to technology and operations. It's they who set the agenda—we're just lucky enough to be welcomed to observe as academic researchers. And an interesting pattern has arisen since the event started in 2016. By far, the two most intensively covered topics each year are data and innovation. At the onset, data got more air-time and focus. But the pendulum has gradually swung the other way: innovation has become the topic that's consistently grabbing most attention.

That annual Stanford event is now a chance for leading players within the institutional investing world to showcase some of their biggest wins in innovating. The projects presented are highly inspiring. For instance, a major sovereign wealth fund demonstrated how it's using natural-language processing technology among its quant-research teams to let them extract deeper insights from dense textual documents. And a large public pension fund treated attendees to a case study about how it's leveraging machine learning to gain hundreds of person-hours in efficiency, by automating several quality-control processes in its back-office functions. These outcomes are clear examples of the stellar increases in technological capabilities that innovation can enable.

But these case studies also make clear that innovation must always be thought of as a perpetual process, not a destination. And that process always has two parts: discovery (i.e., finding or inventing new solutions) and implementation. These are both necessary for innovation to succeed as a whole. Make no mistake about it, in general, neither the discovery nor the implementation of new ideas is an easy undertaking. Removing frictions to both is thereby critical for innovating. And our research has found (perhaps surprisingly) that the chief friction on innovation for many Investors isn't technology. It's culture and behavior.

But that's understandable once one realizes that people are at the heart of innovation. They can be the biggest help or hindrance to innovating, regardless of the state of an organization's tech. That's why lessons and best practices in innovation that we cover here are so people oriented and span four innovation areas: culture, planning and monitoring, sourcing, and teams and execution.

Learning Culture

In all of our work with Investors, we find over and over that the central factor determining whether an organization is capable of serial innovation is the presence of what some practitioners describe as a "learning culture": one that prizes learning, nurtures it, celebrates it, and thrives on it. The two primary hallmarks of learning culture are (1) openness in communication, and (2) methodical experimentation. That is, people in a learning culture feel comfortable in talking freely about new ideas: they know they have a right—and in fact are encouraged—to do so. And they think scientifically, by doing structured, iterative experiments to test ideas, regardless of whether they're required to do things that way.[1]

Having a learning culture is a superpower, but it's not something that gets built overnight. Indeed, many people might at first find the open, experimental mindset of a learning culture to be uncomfortable, particularly if they're accustomed to siloed, bureaucratic organizations. Sadly, from what we've seen, transformation to a learning culture usually can't be rushed, in the sense of forced, top-down change. But there are several pull factors that can be leveraged to help organizations migrate to a learning culture. First, they can take advantage of catalytic events, like regulatory shifts or fast organizational growth, to help reconstitute culture in the wake of change.

Second, senior leadership's vocal support and firsthand involvement can lend a huge hand in migrating to a learning culture. This is especially true when leadership actively participates in announcing, congratulating, and disseminating the organization's successes in innovation, both big and small. Leadership's backing is also crucial for promoting transparency, on which we'll say more shortly. Perhaps the most helpful thing leadership can do, however, is to help *rethink failure.*

"Failure" in finance is often treated as a dirty word. As far as Investors are concerned, that needs to change, because there's typically more to be learned from failure than success. That isn't to say that failure should be sought. It just needs, for the sake of innovation, to become treated as a mechanism for learning.[2] There's a phrase in the start-up world, "Fail small, fail forward," which captures the ideas that (1) the consequences of failure should be contained and controlled (i.e., fit within some reasonable budget), and (2) failure should be productive, in the sense that it's designed to teach the experimenters something specific. Designing experiments to reveal particular insights is an essential part of the iterative paradigm in which learning cultures operate. They hypothesize, run experiments, analyze the results of those experiments, refine the hypotheses and tweak the experiments, . . . and repeat.

An important feature of experiments in a learning culture is not only that they have small downside consequences, but also that they're quick to run. A learning culture should be one that's comfortable with work-in-process solutions (e.g., prototypes and proofs-of-concept) that are effectively rough drafts meant to be continuously improved through iterative experimentation. This small-and-fast way of experimenting epitomizes the atomic focus we described earlier.

Still—small, fast experiments are not learning culture's sole priority. In a learning culture, there's also need for *studied learning*. Not everything can be learned from experiments, nor should it be. People need time and resources to educate themselves on relevant topics (to design better experiments, as well as analyze them). This nonexperimental learning may be through attending workshops or visiting experts outside the organization, online learning, consulting an internal library (digital or physical), or other means.[3]

There's one more aspect of a learning culture we must note here: acceptance of *bimodality*. Innovation is a means to an end for any Investor. Investors also have the (more important) need to deliver significant results from investment activities, which means not every process can be an experiment.[4] Meanwhile, if all experiments had to follow the exact same standards and governance requirements as ordinary activities, then it's likely that few experiments would ever succeed. This calls for special tracks for experimental activities—so long as it appears probable that they will ultimately improve on the ordinary activities they seek to replace. Learning cultures must be tolerant of these two, coexisting modes, which isn't always easy: sometimes a need for efficiency makes experiments take a back seat; other times some of the efficiency in ordinary processes must be set aside to allow for learning. People in learning cultures understand this and are clear on when each mode has priority.

Planning, Monitoring, and Industrializing Innovation

Culture on its own cannot coordinate the experiments needed for programmatic innovation. That's where processes for planning and monitoring come in. While it's certainly true that innovation will wither if starved of resources, Investors must be selective in which ideas and opportunities they pursue in their innovation programs (after all, resources are scarce in the first place!). A few dozen leading Investors whom we have studied make extensive use of *innovation frameworks* for this express purpose. Frameworks of this type are conceptual devices that help an Investor accomplish two things: (1) clarify its goals (over multiple time horizons) in operating an innovation program, and (2) classify candidate innovations (whether specific projects or wider categories thereof).

There are many such frameworks for Investors to choose from (and there's nothing prohibiting them from constructing their own!). Many Investors use more than one. Still, what all users have stressed to us is that it's critical for any chosen framework to align with organizational objectives, resources (whether existing or soon attainable), and the long-term advantages the organization is trying to build. Picking a framework that complements the organization's strengths and highlights how to mend its weaknesses (through innovation) is one of the most pivotal decisions an Investor must make when launching an innovation program. Investors who use these frameworks therefore consider it best practice for senior management and the board to be actively involved with selecting frameworks.

Let's sample the flavor of some of these frameworks and how they're used. A sterling example is the simultaneous use of a pair of frameworks by one public pension fund in Canada. The first helps it position its thinking (and classify candidate projects) within a matrix of markets (on one dimension) and capabilities (on another dimension):

- Markets:
  - existing—markets they already invest in
  - adjacent—markets similar to those they already invest in

- new—markets that are totally different from ones they're already in
- Capabilities:
  - existing—enhancing abilities they already have
  - incremental—adding similar capabilities to ones they already have
  - new—adding totally new abilities

To complement this, the fund also uses a categorization scheme that breaks up innovation areas into four classes, depending on which organizational functions they affect: investing opportunities, portfolio management, internal operations, and the addition of value to existing portfolio holdings. Together, these frameworks help the fund concretely direct its thinking about where within the organization a specific innovation is likely to have an impact, and the degree of change that impact will enable.

Another popular set of frameworks help Investors to settle on their ideal innovation mix. They ask Investors to identify how they'll distribute potential innovation projects across different categories (i.e., create a portfolio of innovations). What categories are appropriate varies across organizations, but we've encountered some examples applicable to most. One is a division between the percentages of innovations that the Investor expects to be *core* (affecting the central functions it performs now), *emerging* (creating new abilities), and *transformational* (significantly evolving the organization's ways of operating). Another is a division across the levels of impact that innovations are expected to have—for example, capability improvements of 2x, 10x, or 100x.[5] And still another division involves specifying the range of anticipated maturities for target innovations—short, near, and long term.

Frameworks are great for planning but, for innovation success, monitoring is also needed. Investors need ways to specify the goals they hope to achieve in an innovation experiment, and ways to measure whether that experiment's outcomes are making progress toward those goals. Multiple Investors assert that best practice monitoring starts with formulating a problem statement. We agree with them. Beginning with a problem statement accomplishes several things at once:

- It's an additional check that the intended experiment fits the overall program.

- It forces explicit statement of hypotheses about what the experiment is expected to improve (i.e., what's wrong in the first place) and how it's expected to do so.

- It compels thinking on, and justification of, how the innovation that experiment is supposed to lead to will fare in the wild (i.e., after live deployment).

The exact form and additional content of problem statements will differ across Investors according to how their individual innovation functions are set up. But, at a minimum, they should address the foregoing points, which serve to frame how the experiment should be monitored. The monitoring protocol for any experiment must also articulate

- what variables will be tracked (these may be objective or subjective),

- what values for those variables constitute a success (ideally, set against some baseline performance of the current solution, or other feasible ones),

- when and how those variables are to be tracked over the experiment's course (e.g.: continually, periodically, or only at its conclusion; directly or by proxies), and

- what experimenters and the organization at large expect to learn from observing those variables' values—both specific to the experiment and for knowledge more broadly.

Investors have indicated to us that an innovation experiment cannot be considered well designed without careful construction of a plan for monitoring it, which should be explicitly written down.

One aspect of monitoring where best practices (and Investor agreement more broadly) have yet to crystallize is on key performance indicators (KPIs) for innovation in general. It can be easy in many cases to identify KPIs for specific experiments, but it's typically tricky to come up with valid KPIs to track innovation progress at higher levels (simply aggregating KPIs from individual experiments can lead to nonsensical results—they might not be compatible with one another—and they don't give a complete picture of the health of an organization's innovation capabilities overall). How best to design organization-level KPIs for innovation is an important open research question.

A further open research question is how to design (what one practitioner colorfully calls) "industrialization processes" for experiments that *graduate*: experiments that have sufficiently matured to the point where they're ready to replace an existing solution (or else become the default for a fully new organizational capability). But transitioning solutions from the special, experimental track to being ordinary isn't always easy. Appropriately industrializing an innovative solution means finding ways to designate responsibility for its implementation and upkeep, as well as to track its ongoing performance (in terms of both the solution's performance, and people's proper use of it).

Sourcing Innovation

Candidate innovations for experimentation don't just appear out of thin air (but we wish they did!). For any Investor's innovation program to succeed in the long run, it needs a strategy for sourcing new ideas. There are essentially two ways to source ideas, and Investors could use both: internal generation and external tracking—either from its own people or from outside the organization. There are a number of different approaches to implementing the latter (and they're not mutually exclusive). One involves using third parties to help match an Investor's innovation objectives with emerging solutions. For example, The Disruption House (which we mentioned earlier) is a start-up that aims to do exactly this by using a matching algorithm. Investors input a template of preferred features for a new capability, and then they're matched to new companies with solutions that meet those criteria. The notion here is that Investors can save time and resources by not developing some innovations internally.

But relying on third parties doesn't necessarily give Investors a comprehensive perspective on the wider developments outside the borders of their organization. It just gives them a view on what companies have cropped up with solutions that may meet some of their needs—in many cases imperfectly so. Being attuned to what's going on in the global innovation landscape is valuable for Investors not only because it can inform their innovation programs; it can also help them pick up on new opportunities and threats to their portfolios.

We've heard several Investors report success in designating members of their teams to track external innovation. This external tracking can take a variety of forms, depending on the organization's needs and ambitions. It can involve picking a target technology or other innovation area that is of interest to the organization, and then tasking designated individuals with studying that target closely. Or, it can take the form of designated persons building close relationships with entrepreneurial and venture communities (we discuss this further below). Either approach can pipe fresh ideas into the organization and can be useful not only in staying abreast of new developments: it can also keep the organization engaged with innovation and inspire its people by making them aware of bold new possibilities that are surfacing on the horizon.[6]

A second way of sourcing ideas is to look inward and tap the creativity of the organization's own people. In many cases, setting up formal channels to do so should take priority over external sourcing, as doing so can help innovation programs be more self-sustaining. It also lets people from all over the organization recognize that they can (and should) take more active, participatory ownership of the organization's "innovation destiny." There are various ways to set up mechanisms that enable the harvesting of internal ideas for innovation. One state pension fund in the midwestern US has a process that allows anyone in the organization to conveniently submit ideas, which are then made visible to the rest of the organization for comment and critique. That fund's leadership recommends giving some structure to submissions (e.g., requiring they include a value statement) to help buoy their quality. That state fund is also notable in that it considers such submissions in employees' annual reviews processes, which indicates to people how much the organization views innovation as a duty for everyone.

We've also seen a number of Investors that make use of innovation committees, that is, special groups that exist to issue calls for (sometimes specific types of) innovative ideas, and then manage the receipt and review of them. Such committees act as gatekeepers that can improve the efficiency of an organization's innovation program and keep tabs on people's overall enthusiasm for it. Some Investors distribute these committees across functions and business units—in other words, they have some members embedded in diverse areas in the organization to allow fluid sourcing and escalation of ideas.[7]

There are two additional best practices in sourcing innovation that our research has identified. The first practice is to factor *momentum* identified by the sourcing process into decisions on which ideas and projects to develop. A given innovation idea or project is unlikely to bear fruit if the people who work on it aren't enthused about it or engaged by it. Getting a sense of what projects inspire people the most is therefore crucial. Measuring this should be a goal for any sourcing program.[8]

Another best practice is to prioritize *continual sourcing*. Gathering innovation ideas from hackathons and annual employee surveys can yield useful candidate innovations, to be sure. But we've found that it's more common for the real wins in innovating to come from systems that enable contribution at any time, not just at prespecified intervals on the calendar. Fluid and continual sourcing is ideal.

Innovation Teams and Execution

The above should make it clear that innovation programs tend to work best when everyone in the organization can contribute and is encouraged to do so. People need to be aware that anyone can be, and everyone must become, an innovator—not just the "creative types" that do hot yoga, sip kombucha, and wax lyrical on the wholesomeness of avocado toast. Nope—innovation must be a team sport.

And there's a real need for fastidious attention to the composition of teams for particular innovation projects. Don't get us wrong, individual experimentation is certainly something that should be promoted and facilitated. It's just that there are limits on what one person can achieve by working alone (except for, say, Reinhold Messner or Alex Honnold).[9] Interdisciplinary research is increasingly showing the merits of building diversity into teams (see, e.g., Page 2007, 2010); and this seems to have especial merit when those teams are pushed to innovate. But there's a balancing act hidden here. Teams need enough common interest to stay engaged with an innovation idea for potentially long stretches (maybe months at a time), but also sufficient heterogeneity to avoid groupthink (Kahneman 2011). There's no universal solution to this, but we've seen some sound practices come to light. One is seeking balance in familiarity with a problem by having a mixture of in-the-weeds experts and people who are (somewhat or mostly) unfamiliar with the specific issue but have relevant skills to tackle it (e.g., folks with deep quantitative abilities or who are exceptional communicators). Having this type of diversity blends the potential for completely fresh reframing of the problem with deep domain knowledge of what's likely to not work (so that dud ideas can be quickly scrapped). We've also heard some Investors that try to cycle new people onto projects at key junctures, to inject novel perspectives and reduce fatigue.

Speaking of fatigue, we'd like to raise a point on dealing with "big" innovation. We've been extolling the merits of atomic and small-and-fast innovation. There will be times, however, when it's necessary for an Investor to trial a large-scale innovation project that involves a sizable fraction of the organization (this might be the case for a transformative idea that is in the final stages of experimentation). Larger experiments can last longer than smaller ones and be more challenging to coordinate, which ups the stress and potential fatigue in running them; from what we've found in interviewing Investors that have run them, communication is more crucial to the success of larger experiments (though it still matters regardless of scale). *Ongoing*, two-way communication is key. Leaders need to report updates at regular intervals (even if there's nothing new to report, and they're just repeating a previous status). Stakeholders and others affected need to know what's going on and that they're not forgotten about! Investors we've spoken to have reported the best results come when regular messages are delivered by a senior leader (preferably the same person or people each time), and that there's a (respectful and informative) lightness to the communication—such as taking the form of a humorous blog or video update on an internal wiki page. On the flipside, anyone affected by or curious about such large-scale experiments should know precisely who to go to with questions or suggestions.

Making Space

We simply can't reiterate enough: long-term Investors need to see and treat innovation as a process. And any process needs inputs. After all, that's what processes do—transform inputs into outputs. We've stated a few key inputs to innovation above, including ideas, motivated people, and culture. But these alone are likely to starve innovation. They might suffice for sporadic innovation, but any effort to make innovation programmatic in the organization will require additional resources. In short, innovation needs to be given permanent space in the organization by way of space in the resource budget. Among the additional resources programmatic innovation needs are time, money, expertise, and transparency.[10] When innovation isn't allocated official space in the resource budget, it can get crowded out by the needs of ordinary processes, which may have more immediate payoffs.

Fortunately, we've found that a few forward-thinking Investors are steadily adopting some ingenious approaches to preserving space for innovation. Many of these are forcing mechanisms to create and maintain space to innovate, and are adaptations of techniques used by the world's most innovative organizations, such as Google, NASA, Toyota, and Bridgewater (the largest hedge fund ever). We're thrilled to see this uptake and the commitment to long-term innovation that it reflects. We'll now share some of our findings on how to keep space open for innovation.

Seeding Budget

Something practically all Investors seem aware of is that innovation doesn't come for free. But even when the merits of innovation are clear, keeping space available in the operating budget to support innovation is rarely easy, especially when either (1) funding for innovation is treated as discretionary, or (2) it gets explicitly carved out from individual units' operating budgets. Both of these approaches to setting aside funding can be problematic—they can slow down the approval process, make innovation susceptible to political capture, and make funding decisions overly contentious (i.e., create scruples about *how* ideas get funded, rather than what gets funded).

For these reasons, several Investors have begun using board-approved *seeding budgets* for funding innovation. These are explicit allocations that are determined up front during the budgeting cycle and cannot be repurposed for activities other than innovating. Clearly, scales, sources, and specific coverages of seeding budgets will vary, but they seem a universally sensible space creator.

Time

Time is among Investors' scarcest operating resources, which is somewhat ironic: Investors' most powerful resource in investing is time (long horizons), but it's in woefully short supply among the people who make decisions on those investments.[11] That makes setting aside time to innovate tricky. But doing so is necessary, as innovation requires time to

- make nontrivial assessments on how the organization might be improved;
- come up with ideas, research them, and design and do experiments on them; and
- build out prototypes, proofs-of-concept, and other early implementations.

For this reason, some Investors have been allowing (even requiring) employees to set aside prespecified fractions of their calendars as "protected time" for innovation-related activities only. This *X-time* approach (X is the percentage of time per week or month reserved for innovating) is meant to mirror Google's 20 percent policy, whereby employees are expected to spend one-fifth of each week innovating on projects they find meaningful, aren't part of their ordinary work, and that they expect will eventually deliver valuable solutions. Gmail, Google News, and AdSense—which are among Google's most recognizable and used services—were all hatched out of this policy. Many Investors cannot, of course, allow all their people one day a week exclusively for innovating. Still, the ability to know in advance how much of one's time is guaranteed safe for innovating is helpful.

X-time can be a highly effective way for organizations to ensure innovation doesn't take a permanent back seat to ordinary processes. One potential difficulty with it, however, is coordinating when people take their X-time. Some organizations will have more need for these times to overlap than others (the same goes at the project level). Yet having large segments of the organization simultaneously taking big chunks of time *not* working on ordinary processes has the potential to be too disruptive. There's at least one Investor out there that's remedying this problem by suggesting (and planning to mandate) that a fixed percentage of every meeting be reserved for innovation activities (e.g., designing or reviewing outcomes of experiments, brainstorming). That setup creates some potentially helpful dynamics for meetings in general—in terms of who meets with whom, how often, and for what duration. We're keen to see if other Investors adopt this idea.

Goals and Incentives

Kaizen is a mechanism that can help preserve both time and goal resources for innovation. What, pray tell, are "goal resources"? They're simply acknowledgements of the fact that people can't handle trying to reconcile too many goals at once without becoming overloaded and prioritizing poorly among them (Kahneman 2011). But it's not just the number of goals that matters; specificity also plays a part. Too many vague or nonspecific goals take up more goal resources than targeted goals (the latter have clear measures of success that make it easier to identify ways to reach them).

The practice of *kaizen*, which has roots in Japanese manufacturing and was famously popularized by Toyota, preserves space for innovation by forcing it down to the task level (there's atomicity again!). One can think of *kaizen* as supporting microinnovation, as it entails a person identifying very specific inefficiencies in her activities or workflow, coming up with a hypothesis on how to improve, and then testing out that hypothesis. *Kaizen*-level innovations are meant to be things that can be implemented within a single day, or at most a week. They therefore absorb very little in goal and time resources, but cumulatively can add up to big gains in how efficiently the organization operates, which is one of the focal priorities for innovation. A key here is emphasis on communication: results of *kaizen* experiments are meant to be reported to others, such that the sum-total of an innovation's impact across the organization (if it's transferrable to other areas) can be substantial, even if the local impact where that innovation started out was only relatively small.

Kaizen is also an efficient mechanism for generating space to innovate, in the sense that it creates direct incentive-alignment for innovators. Those that engage in microinnovations under it are also (usually) the same people that most directly benefit from any performance enhancements that are generated.[12]

Expertise

Expertise is one of the most precious resources long-term Investors possess and distributing it in an effective manner is a cornerstone of good governance (Clark and Urwin 2008). As we've noted above, deep domain knowledge can be a vital form of expertise in innovating, but this expertise is often also in high demand from usual processes and activities. We've heard time and again that an obstacle to innovation for many Investors is that they "can't spare the talent." This mentality has to be squashed, but there are also points where an Investor might not have the requisite expertise in-house to push forward an innovative idea or experiment. In such situations, one Investor has suggested that there are three possible resolutions: relevant expertise must be either "built, bought, or borrowed." That is, it can be cultivated internally via research and education, which can be helpful in the sense that it remains in the organization thereafter: it thus gets amortized over time. But building expertise in this way can be a slow process and result in false starts for experiments.

"Buying" expertise mostly entails hiring experts for short durations (e.g., consultants). That can be expedient, but often is expensive. So, building is often cheap but slow, whereas buying is usually costly but quick. What about borrowing?

"Borrowing" here largely refers to seconding of expertise from peers (e.g., inviting some of their personnel for a few meetings or a visiting stay to share their expertise). We've heard a few Investors express enthusiasm for this sort of arrangement, but we aren't aware of it occurring systematically in practice. We definitely think it deserves exploration in the future, given how it's likely to be cheaper than buying expertise but faster than building it. Below, we'll discuss some further benefits to innovation from interorganizational collaboration among Investors. For now, suffice it to say that access to the right expertise is imperative for creating space to innovate.

Transparency

Perhaps the hardest behavior to cultivate in transitioning to a learning culture is trust. For such a culture to function at its best, people need to feel comfortable giving and receiving honest feedback and critiquing one another's thinking. Of course, such feedback and criticism should be delivered in respectful ways. Nevertheless, it's often a real challenge to get people comfortable with saying and hearing "You're wrong" without emotional attachment. But it's this raw honesty that allows a learning culture to reach its full potential. This fact was recognized by Ray Dalio (2017) when he launched a policy of "radical transparency" in his hedge fund, Bridgewater.

Radical transparency involves creating a work environment where people aren't afraid to "pop the hood" on one another's thinking and press for explanations of the data and logic behind others' assertions and conclusions. Understandably, many people find this mindset intrusive, even threatening (it can trample the ego—it's unsurprising that most of the people who leave Bridgewater do so shortly after joining). But radical transparency isn't based on confrontation: it's designed to get people to share resources (their information and perspectives) and use resources (their thinking) more efficiently (Gino 2017). Radical transparency is thereby a way to create space for innovation in an organization by spreading around cognitive awareness, which, in the long run, can generate more time (by cutting out inefficient thinking) and expertise (by distributing sound thinking). We don't know of any Investors currently using this method. We do, nonetheless, admire its potential.

Physical Space

Creative companies, such as Facebook, Google, and Twitter (along with most start-ups in Silicon Valley that've gone through more than a couple rounds of fundraising) famously spend a lot of energy (and money) on the physical spaces in which their people work. That's because the layout of work space can significantly impact people's productivity, stress, and—most importantly—their patterns of interaction. Each of these entities has their own unique flair in how their office space is configured, but most follow a basic formula: have lots of space for people to gather privately (e.g., meeting rooms), have most space be dedicated to people working collaboratively and openly (e.g., open floorplans, side-by-side desks rather than cubicles), and keep ample room for people to have quieter one-on-one conversations (e.g., breakout corners). This formula respects a basic fact about innovation: it flourishes when people's ability to connect with one another is uninhibited by space, which promotes communication, transparency, and cooperativity (all crucial in innovation).

Many Investors certainly can't reconfigure their offices to look like Uber's. Still, most can repurpose and dedicate some physical space to innovating. This might mean converting a meeting room, part of a cafeteria, or corridor. It could mean putting some comfy seating in unused corners or a green space outside. It may even mean letting people know that it's *okay* to regularly take (innovation-centered) conversations to the sandwich shop across the street. In whatever way it can be achieved, giving people some dedicated space for innovation is one of the best ways for an Investor to immediately and positively promote innovation. It's down to psychological forces that underpin innovation: people must feel *safe* when speaking their minds and suggesting fresh ideas that may initially sound silly. Instilling a learning culture is in no small part about getting people happy with the practice of opening up. Giving them space in which to feel safe in doing so can pay stunning dividends in growing a learning culture.

Innovation Partnerships

There's no reason Investors' innovation spaces (in the overall resource sense) should be confined to their organizations alone. Some of the most striking innovations we've seen have happened when an Investor makes the bold choice to partner for innovation. Partnering to innovate makes sense in many ways, including creating economies of scale and scope, sharing labor, and mixing perspectives. There are two types of innovation partnership for Investors that we've seen work well in practice: partnership with start-ups, and partnerships with one another. We'll discuss both.

Start-Up Collaborations

The build-versus-buy mindset that has historically been pervasive among institutional investors is straightjacketing. It presents an unnecessary dichotomy that's resulted in what we've called the "buy bias," whereby Investors build their own technologies and solutions only as a last resort. But buy-build isn't a binary choice: it's a continuum.[13] Start-ups can help Investors capitalize on that.

Modern start-ups are revered for their innovativeness and long-term Investors have much to learn from them.[14] For example, start-ups can teach Investors a lot about being agile—especially how to hone experimental, iterative processes for innovation. Indeed, one Canadian Investor has embraced the start-up mentality in its innovation program, by enshrining it in the mantra, "Ideate, incubate, scale." That's superb! But Investors can push the envelope even further than just emulating start-ups.[15] They can borrow start-ups' best characteristics by partnering with them.

How should such partnerships work? There's no single right answer, but we can point to one arrangement that we've seen work encouragingly well. It involves a joint project undertaken by a Pacific Rim pension fund and a Bay Area start-up (we'll just call them Fund and Start-up, for the sake of convenience and maintaining anonymity). Circa 2016, Fund wasn't content with its capabilities for analyzing the liquidity in its investment portfolio. Off-the-shelf solutions didn't meet its needs, and spreadsheet-based solutions were too ungainly, in light of its portfolio's high complexity and the many plans it offers to members. It needed visualization and simulation tools that didn't exist. Meanwhile, Start-up was a young company made up of ambitious software engineers looking to seriously upgrade long-term asset owners' analytical toolkits. They had identified analytics for liquidity management as an area ripe for energized thinking and solutions.

The pair realized they had mutual interests and could help one another: Start-up could assist Fund with its need for liquidity technology, and Fund could educate Start-up on some of the nuances in institutional investing (despite having top-notch engineers, most of Start-up's team hadn't worked with any financial organizations before). They agreed to go on a journey together.

In a matter of months, the pair had in their hands a fully functioning toolkit to graphically analyze portfolio liquidity. Yet the benefits to their partnership had become apparent long before that solution was finally ready and deployed. Fund recognized that it was learning a substantial deal from Start-up on flexibly experimenting: how to "sprint" to a *minimum viable product*, how to do responsive and short-turnaround planning, and how to get and receive feedback to maximize learning from "failing forward" (in controlled ways, of course). Both sides considered the joint project a success and were eager to search out further projects for long-term collaboration.

For its part, Fund had learned as much (possibly more) from snags along its journey with Start-up as it did from what went smoothly. Fund had gleaned insights on not only how its organization could improve its capacity for innovation but also how it could be a more effective partner to start-ups. Among Fund's valuable realizations were the following:

- Investors can't just give start-up partners design specs on what they need, and then expect them to come back a short time later with a finished solution. There's a need to work jointly to better understand the problem, strategize on how to create a solution, and then share feedback on the path to it in a fluid way.

- Along the path, need for mutual respect, trust, and appreciation of one another's cultures is paramount. Barriers to communication should be removed whenever possible, or creatively dealt with if they're immovable (e.g., Fund and Start-up found that they were often held up due to being separated by the Pacific Ocean, so they regularly visited one another to permit face-to-face interaction—their journey together was more than figurative!).

- Plans and timelines are perpetually works-in-progress. Mutual patience and the prioritization of flexibility are what enable a more desirable result overall.

The Fund–Start-up collaboration was no one-off. It's replicable by practically every Investor—at least those willing to both learn and teach in constructive, long-term partnerships. We find it no coincidence that some of the mightiest superheroes have sidekicks that complement their superpowers. To us, it's clear that start-ups make excellent sidekicks on the mission to technologize.

Peer Cooperatives

If partnering with start-ups creates Batman-Robin type team-ups, then pooling innovation resources with peers is like launching the Justice League, the Fantastic Four, the . . . well, you get the picture. Something that's repeatedly been made apparent in our research is that, although Investors differ in many ways, they share significant commonalities in the problems they face—especially in data, risk management, and innovation. There are occasions when they compete with one another on opportunities, but by and large, they're far better off treating one another as compatriots, amigos, and seriously powerful allies in executing their overlapping missions of long-term asset ownership.

It makes sense, then, to noodle over how they can share innovation space with one another in productive ways. Time and expertise are

perhaps the most obvious among these. There can be enormous inefficiencies in an Investor rerunning experiments and trying to self-
educate when its peers already have the answers it's looking for. Sharing accumulated experiences and knowledge with one another is one
way to expand collective resource budgets and ensure there's more to
go around for innovation. Relatedly, sharing access to one another's
networks—such as start-ups with whom they've worked or knowledgeable entrepreneurs with whom they maintain healthy connections—is
a fantastic way to pool their collective capacities for innovation by expanding the reach of their collective access.

Yet, when it comes to fostering programmatic innovation, there are
other, even more transformative ways for Investors to collaborate with
their peers. One of these lies in monitoring new opportunities—
whether technology trends, management and innovation techniques,
or other evolving phenomena of mutual interest. By taking a divide-
and-conquer approach, each Investor in a collaboration can *go deep*
and build domain expertise in a subject of interest to all, without a need
to sacrifice breadth. Collectivism in cultivating expertise is a resource-
efficient approach to building a very diversified portfolio of durable advantages that can more smoothly adapt over time.

Another direct path to collaboration is cofounding and jointly participating in incubators, pooling resources to create laboratories in
which to grow projects, or even colaunching complete start-ups. Innovation incubators backed by venture capitalists and angel investors
have enjoyed significant success in the past decade (e.g., Y-Combinator,
TechStars, 500 Startups, and Betaworks; these are also sometimes
called *accelerators*). Two Dutch pension funds, APG and PGGM, have
shown, via their joint backing of the Techruption project—which is a
community to help boost promising start-ups in blockchain, AI, and
environmental technologies—that this model can be portable to institutional investing.[16] This is the first case we've seen where Investor-
peers have joined together to back an entire innovation ecosystem. It
shows immense promise, and we hope to see plenty more of it!

CHAPTER 11   SPINNING UP R3D TEAMS

Donning the Cape

In the entire pantheon of comic-book superheroes, one type of caped crusader intrigues us most: the ones that hold down day jobs. Uncannily, the not-so-super alter egos of this unique breed of crime fighter fall into one of two camps. They're either average Joes, like Clark Kent, or in the top 1 percent of the 1 percent, like Bruce Wayne. It's easy enough to see how Master Bruce could become Batman. With the deep pockets of Wayne Enterprises behind him, he's free to build an unmatched arsenal of high-tech gadgetry. Meanwhile, if we didn't know Clark Kent's origin story of having been born on planet Krypton, we'd never guess that he'd be capable of becoming the Man of Steel.

For us, most Investors are Clark Kent. They all have some hidden abilities, but oftentimes need the right setting to allow those abilities to rise to the surface. We've encountered this need firsthand through a series of special projects that we've undertaken with Investors over the past half decade.[1] All of these projects centered around finding ways to more successfully drive innovation within Investors' organizations. And, although each of these cases had its own unique features, there were plenty of recurrent patterns that make what we learned portable to practically every other Investors' own situation. For the sake of both anonymity and generalization, we're aggregating our findings from four such projects into a single set of takeaways and lessons on innovation transformation.[2] To save space, we'll refer to those projects as "Special Projects," and the four Investors with whom it was our great pleasure to collaborate on them as the "Kents."

In each Special Project, the Kents' respective leadership teams knew they wanted to make innovation—specifically, innovation through technology—a core comparative advantage for their organizations. But they also realized their organizations couldn't just morph overnight. After all, none of their funds were starting from blank slates. They all had entrenched cultures, legacy tech systems, and preexisting, long-term portfolios. As such, the Kents needed to build up their superpowers strategically and methodically, all while keeping the proverbial train running on time. The desired Innovation makeovers couldn't be allowed to compromise their day jobs—innovation couldn't get in the way of execution.

Separate internal units were needed to facilitate these innovation makeovers in ways that wouldn't impede the Kents' existing functions. Accordingly, we advised the Kents to build internal innovation teams that combined different aspects of:

- **Red Teams**: purposed squads that are tasked with shaking up an organization's thinking, looking for weakness and inefficiency, and challenging convention[3]
- **R&D Teams**: in-house units in charge of researching and developing novel sets of capabilities, that can follow different rules than the rest of the organization[4]

The ensuing approach to innovation driven by these purposed internal teams is something we've since been calling *R3D*. We'll describe the R3D model in detail shortly. For now, it suffices to say (based on what we've observed so far) that R3D offers a proven way to inject tech-led innovation into organizations that cannot afford to sacrifice efficiency.

Scoping and Defining Success

The Kents were all looking to foster deeper, more programmatic innovation in their organizations. And the most ambitious among them wanted to ensure they could become *perpetually* innovative by attracting external partners (start-ups, peers, and others) that could help them succeed, and that they in turn could help to thrive. But the Kents all realized that any durable transformations would take time. Rightly, none of them wanted to start a long-term trek without first taking their bearings.

From what we've seen, the best way to begin such bearings-taking is by studying internal frictions that could impede innovation. These frictions primarily come from five sources, and all candidate approaches to programmatic innovation must be able to handle them:

1. **Culture**: There are often many deeply entrenched mindsets and practices in Investors' organizations. These can prevent team members from fully committing and contributing to an agenda of comprehensive innovation.

2. **Resources**: The number of people and space in the budget that can be continuously assigned to programmatic innovation is typically small—at least initially. Moreover, some necessary skill set for innovating might not be available in-house.

3. **Conflict**: Innovation programs must confront existing biases, processes, and tool sets. They'll likely encounter significant pushback in pressuring people to relinquish long-established practices and perspectives.

4. **Implementation**: Programmatic innovation is about more than identifying new ways of doing things; it's also about durably implementing them. Worthwhile ideas are often abandoned because of ineffective, unstructured deployment processes.

5. **Visibility**: Most organizations lose desire for programmatic innovation if examples of success aren't delivered along short timescales—the window for a program to prove itself is often narrow. These examples must be visible and understandable to the wider organization, which won't happen if innovation is poorly measured (e.g., due to a lack of clear metrics). Examples of innovation success can also stay hidden if senior leaders never broadcast them. Either way, innovation will struggle to become programmatic if its successes aren't visible across the organization.

But what counts as successful innovation? In general, many organizations fail to suitably define what the purpose of innovation actually is, and what it means in terms of furthering their missions. We thus worked with the Kents' leadership teams to build definitions for success that are tied to the core *functions* that any innovation program should (ideally) serve:[5]

- supporting cultural evolution by seeding curiosity and active exploration of new ideas—whether they originate from internal teams or external parties

- providing space and incentives to imagine, test, and assess disruptive ideas

- continually finding or devising pathbreaking tools that match users' present *and future* needs

- integrating the organization into the wider innovation community through constructing a network of partners (including start-ups)

The Kents' leadership teams painstakingly dissected these functions and conferred with experts on how to convert them into concrete goals. They met with entrepreneurs, venture capitalists, academics (including us), and others to listen, learn, examine their logic, and ensure that nothing had been overlooked. After all that rigor, they were each able to construct their own definitions for success.

Next, leadership at the Kents used their respective definitions for successful innovation to specify principles that the innovation teams they were designing should uphold. Four points of commonality emerged across these sets of principles, with four requirements for innovation teams:

- **Investor-relevant**: innovation teams need to be grounded in the reality of the organization—they are innovating to better empower investment teams, not just for the sake of innovation itself.

- **Willing to fail**: innovation teams must accept and manage a controlled rate of failure to facilitate learning—which is needed for deep innovation over the long term.

- **Ambitious**: innovation teams' visions for future capabilities must be bold, even if steps they take to reach those visions are through small increments.

- **Strengths-centered**: innovation teams must prioritize efficient innovation by concentrating first on leveraging the organization's current strengths.

After articulating definitions for success and principles by which innovation teams were to abide, the next step for each of the Kents was to find a clearer road map to their destinations.

Charting the Mission

For each Kent, it quickly became clear that their innovation teams' primary task, at least initially, would be bridge building—to link up internal priorities with emerging innovations from the wider technological ecosystem (not just in institutional investing, or even finance, but overall). What the Kents needed, then, was a framework for marshalling their thinking on steps to construct those bridges. To that end, we introduced the Kents to the R3D framework.[6]

While only one of the Kents has launched a true (per our verbatim description) R3D team, they all adopted the core tenets of R3D to varying degrees. The overarching idea of R3D is to merge the purposes and methods of Red Teams with those of R&D Teams. The resulting hybrid, the R3D Team, is a task force embedded within the organization that's equipped to seed technology-centered innovation capabilities across the organization. R3D stands for *recognize*, *research*, *reorient*, and *deploy*, which is a sequence of steps that the R3D team should aim to take in injecting innovation into the organization.

More concretely, an R3D Team strives to

1. **recognize** opportunities to improve processes and tools within the organization,

2. **research** the best available solutions to address those opportunities (whether by buying, building, or borrowing them),

3. **reorient** support mechanisms (norms, incentives, communication processes, etc.) to align with the chosen solutions, and

4. **deploy** the selected solutions and ensure their continual function (before repeating the cycle afresh on other problems).

In spinning up their respective innovation teams, the Kents tinkered with the R3D model to develop flavors of it that fit their specific needs and contexts. We think this is awesome! R3D was engineered as a flexible starting point for building embedded innovation teams. Users should absolutely feel free to adapt it.

Building the Team

The Kents now needed to staff their R3D teams. What types of skills and backgrounds would be called for? This is a question that any Investor looking to create a R3D program should ask itself.

Our research shows that, at minimum, any R3D team should contain five skill profiles: Ambassador, Anthropologist, Operator, Visionary, and Technologist. Each of these skill profiles need not reside in a single individual, and the same individual might embody several of these skill profiles. We're convinced, however, that any performant R3D team should have this overall mixture in order to be considered properly staffed to execute its mission. (We also add that some of these skill sets might be supplemented by outside expertise—e.g., seconding personnel from peer Investors, finding expert advisors, or—as a last resort—hiring advice from consultants).

Below, we give a little more detail on each of these skill profiles and what they can contribute.

The Ambassador

The Ambassador's purpose is as a spokesperson and negotiator for the R3D team, as well as a point person for innovation across the organization. The Ambassador must be in touch with current and long-term developments across the organization and be able to verbalize how solutions being worked on by the R3D team can improve them. The Ambassador is responsible for maintaining friendly, trusting relationships between the R3D unit and other parts of the organization, plus advocating for the unit (cheerleading) and keeping open access to all divisions (to help when sourcing problems to solve).

The Anthropologist

The Anthropologist must be an individual that is deeply in touch with culture across the organization. Their contribution to the R3D team comes from keen knowledge of the people dimension of both problems and solutions. The Anthropologist is tasked with being the team's chief identifier of areas in which the organization could improve norms, behaviors, and values, as well as the one who has clarity on how staff in various divisions will react to new solutions (i.e., knowing what issues related to noncompliance or resistance are likely to surface).

The Operator

The Operator must have a firm handle on organizational structure and processes: she or he should have intimate knowledge of the composition, function, and generic workflows of each division in the organization. The Operator should also be closely familiar with the governance and risk-management policies of the organization. More than anyone else on the R3D team, the Operator should know (1) where problems lurk in "the way things are done," and (2) how proposed solutions are most likely to conflict with official or de facto processes within the organization.

The Visionary

This position's remit is to be the chief sourcing agent for new solutions (technology, techniques, organizational structures) from outside the organization. The Visionary is in charge of keeping abreast of the latest advances and trends in technology and management (e.g., through a network of contacts and attention to research). The Visionary must also know of commercial (or other) partners that may aid the organization in implementing new solutions, if needed. A Visionary works with senior leadership to create a road map for what will be required of the organization in the mid- to long-term future. The Visionary also continually scans for candidate solutions, which she or he then filters before presenting them to the R3D team.

The Technologist

The individual in this role is responsible for being deeply knowledgeable about the organization's technological capabilities and infrastructure. She or he should be keenly aware of the target architecture, along with what problems exist regarding data, tools, and other digital resources (or where there is unmet demand for better capabilities in those areas). Apart from familiarity with the organization's current technology, the Technologist should have a very firm grasp of technology more generally—to be able to rapidly assess candidate solutions that the team considers.

Road Ahead and Portability

We are, frankly, astonished at how far some of the Kents have progressed in launching R3D and innovation teams. Of course, their journeys to programmatic innovation are far from concluded. The Kents continue to have growing pains that'll need work. But anything that's first-of-its kind is unlikely to be flawless! We're over-the-moon excited to witness what the road has in store for this intrepid group. And we sincerely hope that other Investors pay heed to their efforts. They're in the vanguard of ambitious-but-grounded thinking on organizational evolution, but we anticipate they'll soon have plenty of company. From where we sit, what they did appears replicable for just about any long-term Investor, so long as that Investor is willing to commit to:

- being unswervingly honest with itself,
- putting in the up-front effort to appropriately frame the complete process,
- recognizing when and where to ask for help from outside the organization, and

- modifying existing frameworks to get the snuggest fit possible for its context.

Wide replicability of the R3D model could lead to a turning point in how Investors think about the whole process of innovating—and shift it from being seen as mysterious and driven by spontaneity to something that's well defined and controllable. That is, the R3D perspective may help transition innovation from being treated as an inefficient process to an efficient one, which would make the whole business of innovating more salable to boards, internal teams, and stakeholders in general.

The emergence of frameworks like R3D that clear a path to more permanent innovation means the winds of change are picking up for Investors—which will help fan their newly acquired capes.

CHAPTER 12   GETTING STARTED

First Steps

Few folks get the privilege of saving the future as part of their day jobs. Doctors and firefighters save lives. If lucky, a pro athlete may save the championship game. And politicians are mostly just trying to save face. But—with zero exaggeration—the people employed by institutional investment organizations go to work every day to chip away at the problem of saving the world as we know it. That said, if you're the COO of a pension fund, then you probably shouldn't be expecting to get your own action figure or star in a video game anytime soon . . . or ever. After all, how many kids have posters of Clark Kent on their walls? Bruce Wayne birthday cakes? Peter Parker pajamas? Real heroes don't always get the publicity they deserve.

The world's going to need increasingly more heroism from every one of its Investors. The runaway train of climate change, unsustainable debt, deficient health care, food poverty, withered social security, decrepit infrastructure, and other global crises is ahead of schedule. Yet it's not too late to slow it down. Heck, it may still even be stoppable! Either way, doing so will demand speedy, drastic action. Painful experience, however, shows that governance, culture, incentives, and most other levers Investors could pull won't do the trick: they couldn't change quickly or significantly enough on their own to make any sufficient difference. Technology, however, could feasibly work.

Not only is technology changeable—technological change is *inevitable*. To even keep doing their jobs as well as they are now, Investors will need to refresh their technology. So why not change technology in ways that will not just make them better than they are now but allow them to continuously get better? Rather than periodically updating their technology to catch up, why shouldn't Investors rethink their entire approaches to technology—so they can get ahead and stay ahead? That possibility, and the achievability of it, is the whole reason we've undertaken the work that culminated in this book. Every step of the way we've realized that Investors can use tech to remake the game they're in. They can have tech become a superpower that plays to their strengths, as well as use it to build new strengths—in culture, governance, innovation, and managing knowledge and risk. They merely need to take the first steps.

But what even is the first step? Throughout the chapters of this book, we've detailed many different tools—analytical, organizational, and technological—to help Investors on their journeys to technologizing. No doubt, there will be numerous steps along that path. What, then, is the first step that should be taken?

Truthfully, deciding what first step to take matters less than its size. And that size should be small. When planning for any long journey, there's an impulse to start off ambitiously and make the first leg a big one. But there's a snare. If that big push fails, then the whole trek's in jeopardy. Starting small is safer. It also speeds up learning. If you're trying to run a 100-meter dash, then go ahead and take big, energy-sapping steps: you only need to travel along a short, straight line. On the other hand, what wins a distance trail-race, where terrain is unstable and the route's twisty? There, you're best off with short, quick strides and lots of momentum—that way, you can continually adjust your balance, but won't go tumbling headlong if a few of your footfalls are misplaced.

In nonmetaphorical terms: pick a small project where technology can have clear impact. Make sure it's one where outcomes will arrive quickly. And try to pick one that can easily transfer its momentum—one that's sure to get others in the organization excited. This is the same secret sauce that's used liberally by the world's most innovative and successful tech start-ups:

1. Choose a problem that's solvable in a short space of time (even if it's only a tiny segment of the grander problem you eventually want to fix).

2. Come up with a plan to solve it that won't be costly if it fails and that will teach you something valuable, regardless of the outcome.

3. Execute that plan.

4. Figure out what went right or wrong (regardless of success or failure) and get people pumped up to try again—whether on the same problem or some new one.

To Investors accustomed to long-wind-up, heavily vetted, and (supposedly) de-risked projects, this sequence may seem discombobulated, even reckless. It isn't. It's just the ideal implementation of the atomic-scale, iterative approach to innovating we've been advocating throughout the book.[1] The whole point of going about the first project in this way is that it sets up the second project, which sets up the third, and so on, and so on.

This iterative paradigm respects the truth that technology is never really "solved." Indeed, *having* appropriate technology is only a minor element of what it means for Investors to become technologized, which is really more about *being skilled with* advanced technology—in terms of finding it, analyzing it, deploying it, maintaining it, and innovating with it. As with any deep skill, proficiency of this sort takes focused practice. Iterative approaches are what enable that practice in ways that benefit the organization over both the short and long hauls. Iterative approaches are the way to progressively build an entire technology program and infuse innovativeness across the organization—from the bottom up. And they're faster and more surefire than top-down attempts.

There are several other pointers that will be valuable for Investors' first steps on the road to technologizing:

- **Start with low-hanging fruit**—pick a project where technology is likely to deliver a relatively quick and easy win; *do not* try to take on too much at once.

- **Ask around and take stock**—in coming up with a plan, check attitudes and enthusiasm for the project (and for technology in general) of people across the organization; be studious in examining what resources can be brought to bear.

- **Set an aggressive deadline**—don't wait until things are perfect: pick a tight but achievable date by which the plan must be put into action and its outcome realized (if not the final outcome, then the intermediate results on which it'll be evaluated).

- **Measure success**—make sure success is clearly defined with objective ways to measure it that are agreed upon in advance (ideally, these will also reveal ways to improve—thereby baking in learning from the get-go).

- **Reserve time and space**—block off ample time for people who're involved to work on the project and, if possible, try to find space where everyone can do so face-to-face, to facilitate interaction (note: the first step should *never* fail as a result of coordination issues or people not having time to work on the project).

- **Interview people**—look for expertise on the problem and the candidate solution and try to capture that know-how in detailed, structured interviews with experts—whether those experts are in-house, in peer organizations, start-ups, academia, or elsewhere.

- **Seek allies and patrons**—even when individuals in the organization might not be directly involved in the project, try to earn their support and interest; aim to have at least one or two very senior individuals sponsor the project (e.g., give their open approval, offer resources from their unit, or agree to watch over it).

- **Be open, vocal, and energized**—don't cloak the project in secrecy or withhold details on it from anyone in the organization;

publicize its existence, purpose, and progress wherever possible across the organization and solicit volunteers (even if just for feedback). Above everything, be extremely enthusiastic in all communications about the project, irrespective of how it's going.

Any project that abides by the guidelines above will effectively be bulletproof: it will succeed even if it fails. How's that? Well, if it succeeds, it can be held up as evidence: "Yes! We CAN do this!" and "We OUGHT to do more of this . . . gobs more!" On the other hand, if it fails, it will have succeeded in creating a *launchpad*—a documented, legitimate basis for saying, "We *should* have succeeded but weren't able to *this time around* because [fill in the blank with what was learned]. However, if we make these specific changes, then our findings indicate we can do far better!" If the first failure—a.k.a. learning experience—wasn't costly, then it'll be hard to refuse another iteration (assuming it, too, isn't overly costly). Thus, under this setup, success isn't a matter of *if* but *when*.

We guarantee that any Investor willing to dip a toe in and try its first splash this way will be pleasantly surprised on two fronts: (1) by the enthusiasm that percolates up, once even a moderate amount of momentum is gained; and (2) how little demonstrable success will be needed to gain that momentum. The trick to the whole shebang is to *just keep swimming*: check the flight manual, talk to people, ideate, test, and repeat. Simple. Doable. Replicable. That's pretty much the formula for saving the world.

Partnering

It's at this final point that most scholarly books on applied topics offer some "glimpse ahead" via a hand-wavy vision of the future that hasn't been brought up earlier in the book. Thus, one might expect we'd use this final word to mention something like quantum computing or call for more regulatory support for Investors. Nope. We're just going to repeat ourselves: the future of technology for Investors, and institutional investing itself, will involve new ways of partnering—especially with peers and start-ups.

Quite understandably, it's a challenge to build deep skill with technology by doing so alone. That, in part, is why so many Investors have relied on other parties—external asset managers, incumbent vendors, and consultants—for their technological needs. Yet, as we've shown again and again, those have never been genuine, reciprocated *partnerships* because they haven't helped Investors to develop skills with technology. All they've really built are dependencies for Investors.

Technology partnerships with peers and start-ups are an entirely different type of critter. They're terra incognita for most Investors, and that can be off-putting for organizations that aren't used to trailblazing or detouring from convention. But it makes sense to do things substantially differently when those things are far more favorably aligned with your interests than is the status quo. It's what any prudent person would and should do.

Most Investors won't have had much prior experience in partnering with either their peers or start-ups. We recommend they follow exactly the same first-step prescription for technology projects that we've spelled out above. Start with small, straightforwardly solvable problems. Use them as a chance to learn about partners. Be open and—especially—practice active listening. Carve out protected time to work together and do as much of it as possible in person (at least for the first go-around). Don't start off by treating such joint projects as one-offs: approach them as chances to acquire lifelong collaborators. After all, although superheroes can go it alone, they're almost always better off with trusty sidekicks. But they're even better with equally (super)powerful allies.

It's HERO time.

APPENDIX

Flyovers of AI and Blockchain

This brief appendix is for the curious reader who might wish for a stronger grasp of what AI and blockchain are and how they work. What we provide here is meant to give a flyover, high-level view of fundamentals behind modern AI and blockchain. Our approach isn't technical but should still equip a reader to hold her own in any casual discussion about either of these technologies—whether it's with techies or to show off at Sunday barbecues.

AI can be confusing. A big part of this confusion comes from its breadth: "AI" can describe a vast assortment of algorithms that intelligently perform tasks.[1] What counts as AI is therefore determined by how intelligent performance is defined—and there's no universal agreement about what that definition is! Some experts argue that logic-based algorithms or algorithms that retrieve hard-coded facts about the world count as intelligent performance. When people nowadays talk about AI, however, they usually aren't referring to algorithms that are solely hard coded. They typically mean (whether they realize it or not) algorithms that can adjust themselves through experience, that is, that can *learn.* This subset of AI is generally called *machine learning* and entails a wide set of algorithms that share a special property: their performance on relevant tasks improves as their experience grows—without significant human intervention (Abu-Mostafa et al. 2012).[2] "Experience" mostly comes in the form of data, which explains why machine-learning algorithms are so famously data hungry: they generally perform better with more data, but their incremental improvement from adding just a small amount of new data also tends to be small—so they need large amounts of data to do well.

Yet it's not just more data that matters. Data that's more representative of the problem that the machine-learning algorithm faces matters at least as much. That's because machine-learning algorithms tend to be lazy: they try to find any pattern in the data they're given to improve their performance. Sometimes these patterns are only spurious; other times they're due to biases in the data sets that are fed to the algorithm (e.g., due to that data not being representative of the problem at hand). For example, consider a machine-learning algorithm that's supposed to distinguish dogs from cats. If it's only shown examples of striped cats, then it might take a shortcut and simply use the presence of stripes as the chief way to tell dogs and cats apart (most dogs don't have stripes).[3] Hence, if it's shown pictures of unstriped cats, then it could be expected to classify them as dogs. Being able to effectively *generalize* to never-before-seen data—identify unstriped cats as feline—is largely seen by AI researchers as the Holy Grail for AI: *general* artificial intelligence that can gracefully move from domains in which it has experience to those in which it has little or none, just as humans do.[4]

Right now, the shortest route to general AI appears to be through using a breed of machine-learning algorithms that are collectively called *deep-learning algorithms* (often referred to simply as *deep learning*). Deep learning is inextricably tied up with artificial neural networks (ANNs): adaptive algorithms that are able to represent extremely complicated functions.[5] The gist of ANNs is that they construct complicated functions by nesting simple functions inside one another, with the parameters of each function inferred from data fed to the ANN.[6] That is, an ANN's goal is to take a set of input data points (e.g., images, text, time-series) and identify a function that gives the best possible output (e.g., distinguishing dogs from cats, determining whether a movie review is positive or negative, or predicting the next change in Bitcoin's price). ANNs are called "deep" (and therefore are used in deep learning) when many simple functions are nested inside one another (i.e., there are many *layers* in the ANN—possibly dozens or even a few hundred). Presently, most major advances in AI come via deep learning. Hence, when people are talking about "AI" or "advanced AI," they're probably referring to deep learning.[7]

There's one aspect of deep learning we need to flag as crucial for long-term investing: the *interpretability* of deep-learning algorithms. These algorithms are notoriously difficult to train: in the process of finding good-fit functions for input data they're shown, deep-learning algorithms can sometimes go astray and give unintended or poor results. Avoiding such cases (or otherwise improving performance) usually requires human ingenuity in selecting and adjusting some of the algorithm's attributes, such as how fast it learns, how much it "forgets" over time, and how much it prioritizes parsimony in the functions that it learns. Manipulation of these attributes (which are called *hyperparameters*) is something of an art—although it's increasingly being done by other algorithms rather than manually by people.[8] Anyway, how the overall algorithm behaves as these hyperparameters are being fine-tuned can give valuable indications on *how* it makes decisions—that is, it helps with the interpretability of the algorithm by humans.[9]

An ANN's overall architecture and its associated hyperparameters can be exceedingly complex and difficult to holistically understand (even for AI jocks). Yet, for a long-term Investor, this understanding can be hugely important. Pointedly (and as we discuss extensively in the main text), long-term investing is very much about understanding assets and phenomena that impact their value. Doing so gives Investors an edge over long horizons, especially when such phenomena are stable through time. Much of market behavior, however, is driven by unstable phenomena that last only for relatively short periods—so finding and assessing long-term stabilities is a core part of every long-term Investor's job.[10]

Deep learning and other advanced-inference tools can help identify stabilities. But understanding whether these stabilities are genuine or not can sometimes require a user to interpret the algorithm itself. This is why interpretability is so crucial—it's a bridge to being able to understand long-term phenomena and knowing what level of confidence should be placed on that understanding. Interpretability is one of the hottest areas of deep-learning research, and new tools are constantly emerging to assist with it.[11] It's far from a solved problem, yet it's something about which technologizing Investors should be aware.

Along with deep learning and other branches of AI, blockchain is one of the most attention-grabbing technologies to recently become available to Investors. It's just over ten years old, but it's already packing a hefty punch in terms of impact on the financial-services industry and beyond.[12] Assuredly, there's lots of hype around blockchain. It's been claimed to be capable of disrupting practically every industry under the sun. To knife through such claims and separate the valid ones from those that are exaggerated, it's helpful to have a command of some blockchain basics.

Blockchains are also called *distributed ledgers*—for good reason: they're blocks of records that are sequentially organized (i.e., chains of blocks) so that they collectively comprise a ledger of transactions over time.[13] Such ledgers are "distributed" because copies of them aren't controlled by only one operator.[14] Instead, they're spread across multiple (sometimes very many) operators who must come to a consensus on whether or not a given copy is correct. The ease with which operators can reach such a consensus is a product of the (elegantly simple) structure of the blocks that create blockchains—as are many other desirable properties of this technology.

Generally, each file or block in a blockchain contains data that's meant to capture the status of a system (the quintessential example is ownership of a cryptocurrency, e.g., Bitcoin). Every block's data also contains a reference to the block that immediately precedes it in the chain. All of this data is then passed through an encryption function (i.e., *hash function*) that produces a unique identifier for the block, which then becomes stored in the data of the next block once that's created.

An important property of a block's identifier is that it changes whenever any data in that block is altered.[15] Having this property means that if any data anywhere in the chain is altered, then the change cascades downstream to every other block, which makes catching alterations, such as tampering, very easy. (The fact that copies of a chain are shared across many users increases the likelihood of changes being detected and reconciled.)

An essential ingredient of blockchains that isn't part of their architectures is an incentive mechanism.[16] To function properly, most blockchains need to motivate operators to verify whether the data contained in a new block is correct before it's added to the chain (other users can instantly tell whether data is consistent across the chain; but it's harder work to tell that the data in a given block is *accurate*). This is where cryptocurrencies became instrumental to blockchains. Entities that are first to verify data in a new block are typically awarded some unit of cryptocurrency, such as Bitcoin, for their efforts (usually, this reward can be revoked if their verification turns out to be mistaken). Bitcoin and blockchain are therefore circularly related: the initial purpose of blockchains was to track Bitcoin ownership, but they also needed to be able to award Bitcoin in order to even function!

The usefulness of blockchains for Investors extends well beyond tracking cryptocurrencies, although there's still often a need for cryptocurrency to motivate entities to validate transactions. The genuine value of blockchains for Investors comes from their ability to both steer and govern behavior outside of their own organizations. Each of these ends is served by blockchain's capacity to support *smart contracts*: agreements structured as code that execute when specific conditions are met (much as any other contract does). Smart contracts have a staggering number of potential uses. They can be set up to reward a forecaster who makes more accurate predictions than others. They can be used to pay fees to external managers only when particular performance criteria are met. And they can serve as more flexible surrogates for options and derivatives, along with a host of other applications.

NOTES

Introduction

1. The more widely recognized *Hercules* is the Romanized version of the Greek demigod Heracles.

2. Our calculations (with help from colleagues in Stanford's Global Projects Center) put the value of total assets managed by all Investors worldwide as *at least* US$70 trillion—but very likely significantly more, depending on where one draws the line on who counts as an institutional investor, and exactly what capital gets counted as managed by them.

3. As we'll describe later in this chapter, a flight manual is a document that contains the necessary information to *safely* operate a specific aircraft.

4. Short-termism is a well-documented bias not just in institutional investing (see, e.g., Clark, Dixon, and Monk 2009) but also in human psychology and behavioral economics generally (where it sometimes goes by many other names, such as *myopia* and *hyperbolic discounting*; see Laibson 1997; Tversky 2004; Kahneman 2011). All of these notions are unified by the idea that people and institutions have a tendency to focus on near-term outcomes more heavily than they optimally should.

5. Recent research indicates the number of entrepreneurial hubs and start-up communities is expanding geographically, especially outside the US, which means that a growing number of Investors will have such resources in their own backyards— and so could potentially embrace this as a native advantage. See Florida and Hathaway 2018a, 2018b.

6. After all, at the macroeconomic scale, innovation is supposed to be the engine of capitalism, with technology as fuel!

7. This estimate is based on the annual 10-K documents filed by each of these companies with the SEC for the financial year of 2018.

8. Buffett believes *The Intelligent Investor* is "by far the best book about investing ever written" (Graham 2006, ix).

9. Flight manuals do contain plenty of in-text references to parts of preceding sections that are additionally informative. Our book does likewise.

10. This project has uniquely benefitted from hundreds of practitioners sharing countless insights with us—many under an understanding of anonymity. We therefore follow a long-established approach in practitioner-facing realms of social science and retain only the summary messages from our many interviews and other close-dialogue interactions with these research subjects (see Clark 1998). We make specific identifications of our subjects' organizations only where doing so has justified explanatory benefits and there is explicit approval by that organization for our doing so.

11. Although it may be lacking in personality, we'd go so far as to say that AlphaGo has the makings of a superhero. True, clobbering humans at board games isn't saving the world—but "solving intelligence" (which is DeepMind's stated aim) for the betterment of humanity certainly seems to be! In specific, DeepMind is targeting breakthroughs in medical research with some of the insights learned from building the AlphaGo system.

12. On this last achievement, see Silver et al. 2017.

13. Quotations in this paragraph are taken from Metz 2017. For those unfamiliar with go, master-level players receive *dan* ratings on a scale of 1 to 9 (with 9 being the top rating). A 1-dan rating is the equivalent of a martial-arts blackbelt.

Chapter 1

1. Indeed, it's a cardinal sin in change management to take a "Markovian" view, i.e., think that it's sufficient to analyze just the organization's current state when creating a strategy for organizational change.

2. Our tour of invest-tech's history will take us to just shy of present day. In Chapter 3, we'll resume this thread and look at current trends in advanced technology in general, not just in invest-tech.

3. These patterns are similar to those found for technology in general by Arthur (2009), among others.

4. One example of this tradeoff of accepting shallower inference for gains from lower data latency is the practice in many high-frequency trading strategies of transacting on binary signals (e.g., yes/no outcomes from political events, or up/down decisions on interest rates stipulated by central banks).

5. This speed-depth tradeoff is a recurring feature across the history of invest-tech: in the past, the two have alternated in terms of which one contributes more significantly to competitive advantages.

6. It's worth noting that, even outside the tech domain, the field of investing is younger than finance, even though both reach significantly far back in human history.

7. This isn't to say that low data latency has been mostly valueless across invest-tech's history. It's just that there have been steeply diminishing returns to any incremental effort in building speed-based advantages—too steep for many to be interested in them.

8. Brother Pacioli is widely considered the "father of accounting."

9. Of course, new users of double-entry bookkeeping may have seen an initial decline in efficiency, until becoming accustomed to the approach.

10. One major pension fund we've studied has conducted a "spreadsheet audit" in its organization. It estimates that 95 percent of its analyses are done in Excel, and that almost 90 percent of all its spreadsheets contain some errors (of varying severity). It also calculated that its junior and midlevel analysts spend about 30 percent of their time transposing data to spreadsheets and modifying it therein. That's scarily wasteful.

11. This confinement to static data, however, appears to be changing with efforts by Microsoft, Google, and other providers of more conventional spreadsheet software to integrate linked data fields. In terms of restricting analyses, it is utterly infeasible to build and efficiently run any sort of sophisticated artificial neural network by using only Excel.

Chapter 2

1. At the time of writing, that Investor is in the process of just such an upgrade.

2. "Superiority" of third parties in using technology and innovating can, therefore, easily become a self-fulfilling (and, more worryingly, self-sustaining) prophecy.

3. Put differently: comparing how two Investors use and interact with tech isn't ever an apples-to-apples comparison.

4. The argument here becomes somewhat subtler for technology that enhances internal operating efficiency: although the direct advantages of waiting to adopt may not decay over time, many investment opportunities can be wasted by delaying adoption—which equates to the same sort of evaporation of advantages we noted above.

5. Win-win framing can make projects with reasonable-but-salient tradeoffs look unappealing relative to projects that demand smaller tradeoffs but will likely deliver weaker overall benefits.

6. The latter tendency may be partly justifiable due to significant time discounting, but we are concerned that it may be done excessively.

7. This same bias actually often works against smaller projects when they have equal degrees of uncertainty to larger ones. By nature, larger projects with uncertain value are subject to wider absolute variability in their expected value than are smaller

ones with an equal proportional degree of variability. Yet, if only relative expected performance is analyzed (adjusted for uncertainty), then smaller projects are put on a more equal footing with large projects than is justified, given the fact that the absolute risk posed by smaller projects will necessarily be lower than for larger ones.

8. We are, however, now seeing this change in a few funds (that are diverse in both their geography and other contexts).

9. See Monk, Nadler, and Rook 2016. Our interim work suggests little has changed since surveys in that article were administered.

10. On defensible and defensive data strategies, see Monk, Prins, and Rook 2019. It's worth noting that too few Investors seem to be exploring how to build defensible strategies in sustainability data. We speculate that part of the problem may be that many are locked into conventional asset-class-focused mindsets (we'll sideline that hypothesis for future studies).

Chapter 3

1. Moore's law is an observation-based conjecture about the continuing increase in computing power and speed. More concretely, Moore's law predicts the number of transistors that can fit into an integrated circuit (i.e., computer chip) of fixed size approximately doubles biennially.

2. We must now consider data latency as not just being the speed with which data is created, but also the rate at which totally new types of data are appearing.

3. Examples include the cleanliness of Google's search page and the convenience of using an iPad.

4. The open-source code for the Linux operating system is the flagship example.

5. See, e.g., Reed and de Freitas 2015, Lobo and Levin 2015, Miotto, Kidd, and Dudley 2016, Zoph et al. 2017, and Silver et al. 2016 and 2017.

6. Bostrom 2014 delivers a masterful (albeit at times technical) treatment of this topic.

7. Of course, this isn't so for cutting-edge AI, which still requires well-honed expertise (see Rook and Monk 2018a).

8. Some of these platforms are free to download and use, while others are only available as paid services.

9. It's worth pointing out that an Investor needn't have deep familiarity with *all* areas of AI to command an advantage in it (even AI experts don't know all the details of every corner in the field!). It can suffice for an Investor to be decently versed in a few applications and techniques.

10. Alt-data is actually far from new. Remember (from two chapters back) how our Babylonian friends were measuring the Euphrates 6,000 years ago to better understand fluctuation in commodity prices? They were accumulating alt-data!

11. These examples come from Monk, Prins, and Rook 2019. There's a certain relativity in alt-data that's worth highlighting. Above, we say "alt-data may include" because what counts as alt-data for one organization may not for another—it's all down to what's counted as conventional. Of course, one can talk about different levels of convention, e.g., within a single firm, among competitors in an industry, or across all the entities in every financial market. Our focus here is on Investors, so when we talk about alt-data, we mean data that is unconventional in decision making across the global community of institutional investors.

12. This is true for all data sets, not just for alt-data sets.

13. Tools like Google Docs and Sheets can be considered partial examples of collaboration-tech, as they've got some useful joint-editing capabilities. But they are nowhere near as collaboration-centric as some other available solutions.

14. Slack is an acronym for "Searchable Log of All Conversation and Knowledge." It's a platform heavily used in the software-development and start-up communities.

15. A fascinating feature about Inpher and some of its peer technologies is that they work their magic without having to add any distorting noise to data (i.e., one way to allow another party to do calculations on a data set without giving them that data set directly is to add some structured noise to that data, or else perform a high-level aggregation; but, in doing so, one limits the precision of their calculations—amazingly, Inpher and a few others don't require this!).

16. Helpfully, IFTTT doesn't require any intricate programming for such "recipes" (as it calls them). Users can set them up through a graphical interface, using a process that's approximately as simply as sending out digital calendar invites.

Chapter 4

1. An Investor's opportunity set doesn't just consist of its investment opportunities (i.e., assets that are, or potentially could be, in its portfolio). It also includes opportunities to have an environmental and societal impact, as well as open doors to new capabilities for the organization in the future—that is, the opportunity set can include opportunities to access future opportunities.

2. For well-governed organizations, these ongoing changes to the resource budget are primarily intentional and proactive, rather than uncontrolled and reactive.

3. "Affordable" here is in the wider sense of all organizational resources the technology would affect—not just in terms of cold, hard cash.

4. On governance and data budgets, see, respectively Clark and Urwin 2008 and Monk, Nadler, and Rook 2017. It should be noted that the data and risk budgets are somewhat special compared to the operating and governance budgets. The latter two deal with resources directly: money to run the organization in the case of the operating budget, and resources like expertise, time, and knowledge in the case of the

governance budget. The data and risk budgets, on the other hand, deal with *capacity for managing* resources—i.e., the data budget concerns the organization's ability to manage its data, whereas the risk budget captures its ability to tolerate a specific amount and distribution of risk (see Chapter 8). It deserves mentioning that, historically, enlarging the risk budget has also required increasing the governance budget (at least when increases to the risk budget are done responsibly).

5. Predata is an example of such a platform. It uses a combination of location-linked alt-data and advanced-inference algorithms to deliver focused diagnostics on geopolitical risk—especially at very precise geographic scales.

6. Importantly, by outsourcing a significant fraction of their portfolio management to outside entities, many Investors must spend nonnegligible resources on diligence and monitoring of those entities (especially if they operate active strategies). Doing so taxes an Investor's governance budget. Thus, in-sourcing need not involve a massive increase in the governance budget; it may just require reassigning resources in it—and may even allow an overall reduction to it.

7. Our conceptualization of the risk budget here isn't the amount of variability in returns an Investor can tolerate in its portfolio, as standard definitions for the risk budget entail (e.g., Litterman and Quantitative Resources Group 2003). We'll divulge our "new view" of risk budgeting (which is more tech-centric) in Chapter 8.

8. Since data is, in essence, raw material for information and knowledge, its value can actually be more stable over time than that of information: data is typically more of a multifunctional asset in the organization than information is. Nevertheless, information is still highly valuable to the organization, as we shall see when studying risk management.

9. See Monk, Prins, and Rook 2019 for a more detailed discussion of rivalry and excludability in the context of alternative data.

10. Scarcity is distinct from excludability, although the two are related. Data that are excludable are necessarily scarce, but scarce data need not be excludable. Scarcity is thus somewhat of a weaker property for data than is excludability.

11. Unknown and unknowable knowledge can simply be seen as two degrees of the absence of knowledge, i.e., unknown knowledge relates to something an organization doesn't know it doesn't know; whereas unknowable knowledge relates to something an organization can never know.

12. Taleb refers to this effective emphasis on what one doesn't know (that is, negative knowledge) as "via negativa."

Chapter 5

1. There is no chronological order here—e.g., to become technologized, an Investor needn't check off all three Core Attributes before moving on to Sources of Advantage, or vice versa. The deepest, most durable success an Investor can have in reorient-

ing itself around technology, however, will come from eventually possessing all of these features.

2. That is, they aren't necessarily attributes that will have to be possessed right off the bat for Investors to meet success along their journey to becoming technologized. But an Investor should possess them at some point to maintain success in embracing technology. And the sooner it does so, the deeper that success will be.

3. We later found that management guru Peter Drucker may have originally coined this quip.

4. Still, it should be recognized that such organizations would always be benefitted by better technology.

5. Efforts to *positively* change organizational culture don't usually result in *negative* unintended consequences. Still, unanticipated bad outcomes can and do happen!

6. While we're chiefly concerned about practice in this book, there's a sound rationale for atomic focus in the theory of *real options*. See, for example, Smit and Trigeorgis 2004.

7. Notably, the lower resource intensity of microprojects means that they can often be run in parallel, which shortens overall implementation timelines and accelerates learning—especially if project teams can openly share their experiences with each other.

8. We aren't aware of any Investor that directly mentions tech in its official investment beliefs. Hopefully somewhere there's one that does—and that this'll become a norm soon.

9. See Taleb 2018 for a thorough and insight-filled treatment of the topic.

10. It's also ideally in close touch with the wider community of start-ups, even though its focus is on invest-tech start-ups.

11. This and other results from those studies is further detailed in Monk, Nadler, and Rook 2016.

Chapter 6

1. See, e.g., Bridle 2018 and Kirchner 2010.

2. Note that some data-governance policies put very little responsibility in the hands of end users, which would seem to further erode the need for separating management and governance of data.

3. Describing data as a "process" is really just shorthand for the sum total of interactions that users have with data for the purposes of decision making and generating insight. Explicitly describing data as being a process underscores the dynamic nature of these interactions, and is a more helpful conceptualization than just viewing data as being an input.

4. As with tech in general, we know of few Investors that mention their own data in their investment-belief statements.

5. Knowledge management is also gaining traction. But it's got a way to go until it's given the full emphasis it deserves.

6. This default supposition, however, neglects the fact that much data can still remain unstandardized in organizations that follow a strict dogma of standardization—it simply goes underground and is ungoverned by the system (often residing in rogue spreadsheets). It's called *dark data*. Spooky stuff.

7. Yes, we have heard practitioners categorize data systems in terms of "degrees of anarchy." Turns out there is some quite colorful (and even impolite) language that crops up in systems architecture among institutional investors. Who knew?

8. To avoid confusion: in Chapter 4 we suggested that Investors prioritize analyzing the data and knowledge impacts of new technologies over their impacts on information. The justification we gave is that information is able to answer specific questions, and that data and knowledge are collectively able to address much broader ranges of questions than information alone can. This is not to say that information management is any less important than data or knowledge management. Indeed, much of Investors' performance is dictated by the cumulation of individual decisions they make. Since individual decisions are largely driven by information (and, hopefully, a healthy dose of knowledge), managing information well clearly matters. But the specific information that Investors need over time can change drastically. By prioritizing knowledge and data, Investors should be able to make their decision making and capabilities more robust over the long term.

9. Rather than building data dictionaries from scratch, there are emerging tools to make constructing them far easier (for example, tools offered by the data start-up, Alation).

10. A helpful norm we've heard encouraged by several Investors is *data skepticism*, whereby consumers of any data set are urged to respectfully question and ask for proof about its quality. This mindset helps data quality to become more self-policing in organizations and can be useful for detecting errors in data that might have escaped owners' attentions.

11. We feel a useful ingredient here is that only successful contributions be rewarded, but that contribution be expected.

Chapter 7

1. Of course, obsolescence of database architectures is a somewhat moot point if an Investor significantly restricts what data it uses and tools it uses on that data. But that's the antithesis of every message we're delivering in this book.

2. In software development, a "stack" is the minimal set of all applications and programs needed to make some platform or other program work—i.e., the stack is the collection of components that together enable some larger functionality. Thus, a data-science stack is the set of tools that a data scientist needs to do almost all of her work.

3. The American Film Institute ranks this as one of the top-100 most important movie quotations in American cinema.

4. For one approach to doing this, see Schelter et al. 2017.

5. Think of them as enabling the equivalent of flat-pack furniture for analytical software.

6. Capacity to support advanced inference algorithms is only one dimension to consider in such decisions.

7. Code and text editors such as VIM also flaunt macros. We're guessing that most of our readers would dislike VIM (or already do).

8. While they can be automatically activated, setting them up that way can be very tricky, especially for novice users.

9. Examples include Jupyter notebooks, Google Colab, and Airtable.

10. Inside the organization, repositories such as model zoos could help alleviate this problem.

11. Transparent disclosure: both of us have worked extensively with RCI and both of us have financial interests in it.

12. Some examples include Paperspace, FloydHub, various utilities within Amazon Web Services, and Google Colab.

13. When building deep-learning models, we personally tend to use cloud processing.

Chapter 8

1. The petroleum industry made a significant contribution to development and refinement of real-options techniques.

2. As the winner of a Nobel prize for his contributions to econometric techniques for analyzing risk, it's possible that he knew what he was talking about.

3. This doesn't mean overloaded terms (in specific, *innovation* and *sustainability*) don't matter. Indeed, the reverse is often true. What's more, they matter because they're so intricate, multifaceted, and encompass a great many things.

4. Attribution and benchmarking are often seen as exercises for tracking performance, rather than managing risk. We will be covering why long-term Investors (not just technologized ones) are better off treating them as risk-management functions.

5. Knight's (1921) work was strongly influential for economists' views on risk, uncertainty, and ambiguity during the first two-thirds of the twentieth century. Also see Savage 1954, Ellsberg 1961, and Anscombe and Aumann 1963.

6. Many people think that the mere act of stipulating probabilities pushes a situation from the domain of uncertainty or ambiguity into the domain of risk. It doesn't. But, as we'll see, by using many of the tools of modern finance, one is implicitly accepting that assumption.

7. Of course, if price is the only outcome one cares about, then the distinction between uncertainty and ambiguity is immaterial. Long-term Investors, however, should care about far more variables than just price when owning an asset.

8. Economists often use hyperparsimonious models to focus on some economic feature in order to study it up-close, as if the model were a caricature; see Gilboa et al. 2014. It's often contended, however, that this caricaturing can be taken too far when abstracting away reality.

9. It should be noted that VaR doesn't require normality, but popular implementations nevertheless assume it. See Bernstein 1992 and Markowitz 1999 on the history of VaR as a modern tool of finance. The modern formalization of the efficient markets hypothesis (EMH) uses its own assumption on normality (in the form of the distribution of errors). The roots of the EMH are challenging to trace but seem to have entered mainstream economics through Savage's (1954) popularization of a thesis by Bachelier in 1900. The original sources for the other above-mentioned tools are Black and Scholes 1973; Merton 1973; Sharpe 1964, 1966; Lintner 1965a, 1965b; and Mossin 1966.

10. It's helpful to notice that the above models are not the only ones that could give rise to these "sensible things."

11. See Sheikh and Qiao 2009 for recent empirical evidence.

12. Advantages can be in spotting and constructively adding value, or in avoiding its destruction over the long run.

13. There's terminological subtlety here. Some people see "active investing" as continuously buying and selling assets (especially public securities) to capitalize on short-term price swings (confusingly, so-called passive investing fits this definition, as it entails ongoing reweighting in a basket of assets to match some index). That's not the active investing we're talking about. Another perspective thinks active investing involves continuously *monitoring* investments so that some action can be taken on them if a suitable threshold in their behavior (usually price) is crossed: it's a buy-and-hold approach that permits *infrequent* actions to alter the portfolio when sufficient conditions for doing so are met. This latter type of active investing is what we're talking about.

14. As we'll try to make clear in the following, one can think of the amount of risk allocated to a portfolio asset under this framework as a fraction. The numerator is the strategy-relevant information the Investor doesn't have about the asset. The denominator is the extent to which arrival of that information would be actionable. Increasing actionability therefore reduces the room that asset takes up in the risk budget. Under this perspective, assets in the portfolio that are unactionable are also infinitely expensive (i.e., due to the division by zero), regardless of any information about them.

15. At least four things are worth noting here. First, this interpretation implies that arrival of actionable information frees up room in the risk budget. That seems sensible, and possibly easier to visualize than a lack of actionable information. Yet

emphasizing where information is lacking is a core part of the perspective on risk that we're advocating: it's a forcing mechanism that leads an Investor to deeper understanding. Second, one might argue that this view favors investment in strongly correlated assets. To an extent, that is absolutely true: there are informational efficiencies in this, as learning something about one asset translates into more information about another when the two are correlated. So, all else equal, correlated assets are cheaper in this respect. Still, their ultimate costliness also hinges on *actionability*. Here's an example: Consider two pairs of assets, where each asset in a pair is heavily correlated with the other—except in one pair the correlation is bunched up in time, while in the latter it's spaced out. That is, the former pair tends to move simultaneously, while there's a lag in the latter. The former pair is less actionable than the latter, in the sense that there is some ability to beneficially respond to one asset's movement by acting on the other (which is not as easily doable for the first pair). Third, note that actionability will tend to be reduced whenever other market players can also take action (i.e., when there's the sort of rivalry we described in Chapter 4). Fourth, actionability need not be limited to just buying and selling. As we'll see, there can be other, more valuable actions that technologized Investors may take.

16. This lack of information should be balanced by expectation of higher returns (i.e., one expects more compensation for putting up with a greater lack of information); but the matter of returns expectations lives outside the risk budget—it's not in the risk budget's job description.

17. Some of the ideas in this section extend those presented in Monk, Prins, and Rook 2019.

18. Of course, Investors shouldn't altogether ignore others exiting. Nor should they avoid capitalizing on a false alarm.

19. The International Tsunami Information Center advises: "When the sea begins to drain away, do not go to investigate, but quickly go inland away from the shoreline."

20. Of course, as with any information pipeline, there's a need to have a systematic way to deal with false alarms (i.e., false positives). In the growing field of data science, there are two metrics related to this concept: *recall* (Every time something happens, how many times does our system predict it?) and *precision* (When our system says that something will happen, how many times does it then actually happen?). The difference between these two metrics is subtle but immensely important. We find it odd that many Investors' risk-management systems don't accommodate these terms.

21. The simplest way to obtain such label-derived information is web scraping or use of human-in-the-loop platforms, whether on digital tasks (e.g., Amazon Turk) or physical ones (e.g., TaskRabbit, for getting people to check in-store labels).

22. Summaries of this nature might be considered proto-knowledge.

Chapter 9

1. We don't mean selectivity just in the sense of single assets. We also mean selectivity in the collective composition of the entire portfolio: both the parts and the sum matter (e.g., selectivity in both contributes to *smarter* diversification).

2. A common misconception about organic food is that it's always healthy. Not true. Organic red meat isn't very healthy. Organic is a great place to start, but genuine long-term health comes from knowing what to eat as well as what's in it.

3. Neither of us own, nor ever will own, skinny jeans.

4. See Buettner 2008.

5. To reiterate: we're not fans of asset-class-based allocation (at least when conventional asset-class definitions are used).

6. Processes that start with the market portfolio also follow this two-step recipe, as they usually consider the categories to be down- or up-weighted relative to the market portfolio before they choose any weightings within those categories.

7. Notice that it's hard to get pure exposure to something (or say that you deeply understand it) when you only vaguely specify what that something is in the first place. This, logically, explains the need for sharp specificity in the first step.

8. Furthermore, we're reticent to call long-term realities "themes."

9. That is to say: it's needed if we're talking about exposures Investors can truly use in deriving benefits from their unique advantages. Alt-data is not needed, however, if we're instead talking about exposure to overfarmed statistical factors extracted from conventional financial data (see, e.g., Fama and French 1992, 1993, 2012, 2015).

10. Not to mention the fact that these labels help raise eyebrows when unpronounceable ingredients show up in food.

11. For a given person, it also fluctuates day-to-day: with how much exercise they're doing, whether they're sick, etc.

12. On relational contracts, see Baker, Gibbons, and Murphy 2002 and Gibbons and Henderson 2012.

Chapter 10

1. We'll see next how planning and monitoring systems can help coordinate this experimentation in the organization. Those systems help enforce a scientific, experimental mindset. Yet, ideally, in a learning culture people would feel compelled (as well as motivated) to be scientific and experimental, even without formal requirements that they be so.

2. Integral to a learning culture is a clear delineation of what types of failures are okay (i.e., learning experiences that are a natural part of innovating) and which aren't (e.g., those due to recklessness or sloppy work).

3. It's been widely reported that Facebook's corporate motto is "Move fast and break things." We'd suggest Investors avoid that slogan in favor or "Move fast while

learning things." As we'll touch on below, there should be resources set aside in Innovation programs for employee learning, among other activities that can enhance long-run innovation.

4. To avoid any confusion: innovation and experimentation are about perpetuating the consistency of (strong) results into the long-term future. Consistency and performance in the immediate future mustn't be unduly sacrificed, but there is also a need to invest in longer-term consistency and performance through innovating, which requires experimenting.

5. The Investor that uses this approach claims it mirrors the way many venture capitalists structure their portfolios to contain a few "easy putts," a few "moonshots," and the remainder as "medium bets."

6. There are several consequential decisions in assigning people to monitor external innovation. One is whether they should do so part- or full-time. Another is whether this assignment should be permanent or rotational (i.e., people take turns). A third is where in the organization these assignees should come from (just one unit, or anywhere). These are some important questions that, as yet, don't have complete answers because best practices have not clearly emerged.

7. These embedded committee members are sometimes called "innovation champions," which is a title we support.

8. Another point to consider is not just what projects and ideas stir up initial momentum, but which are likely to maintain it over the lifespan of the experimenting process. For some projects, luster can increase over time, while for others it fades.

9. For those who might be unaware of their accomplishments: Reinhold Messner was the first person to succeed in a solo ascent of Mount Everest (amazingly, he did it without supplemental oxygen); and Alex Honnold was the first person to scale El Capitan in Yosemite by himself without any ropes (in what's called *free-soloing*). Makes us dizzy!

10. Transparency is properly viewed as a governance resource.

11. Wait . . . is that irony? We can never totally remember: that old Alanis Morissette song made us permanently unsure.

12. This is not always the case, especially in non-*kaizen* approaches. Sometimes people who absorb the costs of innovating aren't the same ones that benefit most, which creates externalities that might need to be addressed with incentives to motivate more desirable behavior (i.e., induce more effort by innovators, even though they may not see the majority of benefits). But norms have yet to emerge on what relative weight should be assigned to innovation performance versus ordinary work. In general, how to best incentivize innovation is an open question for research.

13. The buy-versus-build dichotomy is false in more ways than one. Many Investors whom we've researched report that even when they buy an off-the-shelf solution, they usually end up having to tinker with it to fit their specific needs. They regularly end up building even when they elect to buy.

14. Technically, any young business is a start-up. A newly opened mom-and-pop shop is therefore a start-up. We use the qualifier "modern" here to refer to a type of start-up that's surged in popularity and success since the internet-era began: digital-focused start-ups that have an agile, high-growth mindset, learning culture, and are generally built to innovate. Hereafter, we'll just be calling modern start-ups "start-ups."

15. In fact, trying to strictly copy how start-ups work is a bad idea. It's perfectly acceptable to adopt some of their practices and ways of thinking. Yet it must always be born in mind that the two ultimately have distinct missions: start-ups aim to grow quickly, while Investors seek to maximize their long-term performance. One is de-signed to allow for failure, while the other was designed to prevent it. Selectively mim-icking start-ups is excellent; Investors just need to be aware of where to draw the line.

16. See https://www.techruption.org/.

Chapter 11

1. After all, we do work in the Global *Projects* Center at Stanford.

2. The projects from which these summary lessons are drawn were extensive, with each lasting from several months to years. These deep exposures gave us an ultra-high-resolution picture of the obstacles Investors face in unlocking innovation in their organizations—and how they can do so without excessively sacrificing their short-term efficiency.

3. Red Teams are commonly used by NASA, the military, and other organiza-tions that face high-risk/high-reward missions. Although the roles of specific Red Teams vary, they are officially responsible for playing devil's advocate.

4. R&D Teams that are cloistered in this way are often called *skunkworks*.

5. While each of the Special Projects took a (roughly) similar course, they didn't occur concurrently or in concert; they were independent from one another. To cut down on wordiness in the next few sections, we'll limit phrases such as "in each of these four cases" that refer to common occurrences that took place at different times for each project. Readers should be aware, however, that such phrases are implied.

6. See https://papers.ssrn.com/sol3/papers.cfm?abstract_id=3134078.

Chapter 12

1. As we noted earlier, the start-up community would recognize this process as part of an *agile-development* approach.

Appendix

1. Domingos 2015 gives a colorful, nontechnical presentation of many of these algorithms.

2. Although significant human intervention isn't required for machine-learning algorithms to learn, some tinkering and guidance from knowledgeable humans can

often greatly boost their performances; see, for example, Goodfellow, Bengio, and Courville 2016 and Rook and Monk 2018a.

3. In case some canine aficionados in the crowd get picky: yes, dogs with brindle coats can have some subtle striping.

4. Okay . . . perhaps *more gracefully* than some humans do would be preferable. The "generalization problem" typically refers to far more complicated issues than distinguishing cats and dogs—we're just invoking that as a simple example.

5. The importance of complex functions is that every cause-effect relationship in the world can be represented by some sufficiently complex function. The allure of ANNs is that, with enough complexity in their architecture and sufficient data on which to train, they can approximate any function—they could theoretically learn any learnable relationship!

6. ANNs are often described as algorithmic representations of brains. That's a somewhat crude depiction of what they do and how both ANNs and brains work. The core idea behind this supposed parallel is that each simple function in an ANN acts like a neuron that does a basic computation on data that's fed to it, and then passes that computation's output along to other simple functions (i.e., it activates other neurons downstream).

7. In the rest of this book, we'll largely be doing the same.

8. The algorithm-assisted process of fiddling with hyperparameters while a deep-learning algorithm is training is commonly referred to as *automated machine learning* (auto-ML) (or, in more specific cases, *architecture search*).

9. Some regulatory pressures are also de facto requiring interpretability.

10. Some excellent thinking on the hunt for stabilities—and the perils of undetected instabilities—is done by Sornette 2003; Mandelbrot 2004; Diebold, Doherty, and Herring 2010; and Taleb 2012.

11. Gill and Hall (2018) provide a helpful explanation of some of the latest work on interpretable machine learning. See also Voosen 2017 on opening the "black box" of AI.

12. The concepts of blockchain and Bitcoin were jointly introduced in a paper by a mysterious entity: Nakamoto (2008).

13. Luca Pacioli might approve: they implicitly embed some ideas from double-entry bookkeeping.

14. At least, this is the case for most blockchains of value to Investors.

15. This property is a consequence of the sensitivity of the hash function.

16. We won't launch into a slippery discussion here. But we'd nevertheless like to draw readers' attention to the fact that we're not fans of so-called *private* blockchains. They make barely any sense for Investors. Interested readers can find insightful discussion on the few cases when private blockchains might be appropriate in Wust and Gervais 2017.

REFERENCES

Abu-Mostafa, Y.S., M. Magdon-Ismail, and H-T. Lin. 2012. *Learning from Data*. AMLBook.

Anscombe, F., and R. Aumann. 1963. "A Definition of Subjective Probability." *Annals of Mathematical Statistics* 34 (1): 199–205.

Arthur, W. 2009. *The Nature of Technology: What It Is and How It Evolves*. New York: Free Press.

Baker, G., R. Gibbons, and K. Murphy. 2002. "Relational Contracts and the Theory of the Firm." *Quarterly Journal of Economics* 117 (1): 39–84.

Bernstein, P. 1992. *Capital Ideas: The Improbable Origins of Modern Wall Street*. New York: Free Press.

Black, F., and M. Scholes. 1973. "The Pricing of Options and Corporate Liabilities." *Journal of Political Economy* 81 (3): 637–54.

Bostrom, N. 2014. *Superintelligence: Paths, Dangers, Strategies*. Oxford: Oxford University Press.

Bridle, J. 2018. "Data Isn't the New Oil—It's the New Nuclear Power." https://ideas.ted .com/opinion-data-isnt-the-new-oil-its-the-new-nuclear-power/.

Buettner, D. 2008. *The Blue Zones: Lessons for Living Longer from the People Who've Lived the Longest*. Washington, DC: National Geographic.

Clark, G. 1998. "Stylized Facts and Close Dialogue: Methodology in Economic Geography." *Annals of the American Association of Geographers* 88 (1): 73–87.

Clark, G., A. Dixon, and A. Monk (eds.). 2009. *Managing Financial Risks: From Global to Local*. Oxford: Oxford University Press.

Clark, G., and R. Urwin. 2008. "Best-Practice Pension Fund Governance." *Journal of Asset Management* 9 (1): 2–21.

Dalio, R. 2017. *Principles: Life and Work.* New York: Simon & Schuster.

Davenport, T., and A. Spanyi. 2019. "What Process Mining Is, and Why Companies Should Do It." *Harvard Business Review,* April 23.

Diebold, F., N. Doherty, and R. Herring (eds.). 2010. *The Known, the Unknown, and the Unknowable in Financial Risk Management: Measurement and Theory Advancing Practice.* Princeton, NJ: Princeton University Press.

Domingos, P. 2015. *The Master Algorithm: How the Quest for The Ultimate Learning Machine Will Remake Our World.* New York: Basic Books.

Ellsberg, D. 1961. "Risk, Ambiguity, and the Savage Axioms." *Quarterly Journal of Economics* 75 (4): 643–69.

Fama, E., and K. French. 1992. "The Cross-section of Expected Stock Returns." *Journal of Finance* 47 (2): 427–65.

———. 1993. "Common Risk Factors in the Returns on Stocks and Bonds." *Journal of Financial Economics* 33 (1): 3–56.

———. 2012. "Size, Value, and Momentum in International Stock Returns." *Journal of Financial Economics* 105 (3): 457–72.

———. 2015. "A Five-Factor Asset Pricing Model." *Journal of Financial Economics* 116 (1): 1–22.

Florida, R., and I. Hathaway. 2018a. "How the Geography of Startups and Innovation Is Changing." *Harvard Business Review,* November 27.

———. 2018b. "Rise of the Global Startups City: The New Map of Entrepreneurship and Venture Capital." *Center for American Entrepreneurship,* research report, http://startupsusa.org/global-startup-cities/report.pdf.

Gibbons, R., and R. Henderson. 2012. "Relational Contracts and Organizational Capabilities." *Organization Science* 23 (5): 1350–64.

Gilboa, I., A. Postlewaite, L. Samuelson, and D. Schmeidler. 2014. "Economic Models as Analogies." *Economic Journal* 124: F513–F533.

Gill, N., and P. Hall. 2018. *An Introduction to Machine Learning Interpretability.* Sebastopol, CA: O'Reilly Media.

Gino, F. 2017. "Radical Transparency Can Reduce Bias—but Only If It's Done Right." *Harvard Business Review,* October 10.

Gleeson-White, J. 2013. *Double Entry: How the Merchants of Venice Created Modern Finance.* New York: W. W. Norton.

Goodfellow, I., Y. Bengio, and A. Courville. 2016. *Deep Learning.* Cambridge, MA: MIT Press.

Graham, B. 2006. *The Intelligent Investor—Revised Edition.* New York: Harper Business.

Granger, C. 2010. "Risk: A Decision Maker's Perspective." In Diebold, Doherty, and Herring, 31–46.

Kahneman, D. 2011. *Thinking, Fast and Slow.* New York: Farrar, Strauss and Giroux.

Kay, J. 2013. "Enduring Lessons from the Legend of Rothschild's Carrier Pigeon." *Financial Times,* May 28.

Kirchner, L. 2010. "Data Is the New Soil: David McCandless' TED Talk on Visualizing Data." *Columbia Journalism Review*, https://archives.cjr.org/the_news_frontier/data_is_the_new_soil.php.

Kirkpatrick, C., and J. Dahlquist. 2016. *Technical Analysis: The Complete Resource for Financial Market Technicians*, 3rd ed. Old Tappan, NJ: FT Press.

Knight, F. 1921. *Risk, Uncertainty, and Profit*. New York: Houghton Mifflin.

Laibson, D. 1997. "Golden Eggs and Hyperbolic Discounting." *Quarterly Journal of Economics* 112 (2): 443–78.

Lauwers, D., and M. Willikens. 1994. "Five Hundred Years of Bookkeeping: A Portrait of Luca Pacioli." *Tijdschrift voor Econornie en Management* 39 (3): 289–304.

Lintner, J. 1965a. "Security Prices, Risk, and Maximal Gains from Diversification." *Journal of Finance* 20 (4): 587–615.

———. 1965b. "The Valuation of Risky Assets and the Selection of Risky Investments in Stock Portfolios and Capital Budgets." *Review of Economics and Statistics* 47 (1): 13–37.

Litterman, B., and Quantitative Resources Group. 2003. *Modern Investment Management: An Equilibrium Approach*. New York: Wiley.

Lo, A., and J. Hasanhodzic. 2010. *The Evolution of Technical Analysis: Financial Predictions from Babylonian Tablets to Bloomberg Terminals*. Hoboken, NJ: Bloomberg.

Lobo, D., and M. Levin. 2015. "Inferring Regulatory Networks from Experimental Morphological Phenotypes: A Computational Method Reverse-Engineers Planarian Regeneration." *PLOS Computational Biology* (June 4).

Mandelbrot, B. 2004. *The (Mis)Behavior of Markets: A Fractal View of Financial Turbulence*. New York: Basic Books.

Mandelbrot, B., and N. Taleb. 2010. "Mild vs. Wild Randomness: Focusing on Those Risks that Matter." In Diebold, Doherty, and Herrin, 47–58.

Markowitz, H. 1952. "Portfolio Selection." *Journal of Finance* 7 (1): 77–91.

———. 1999. "The Early History of Portfolio Theory." *Financial Analysts Journal* 55 (4): 5–16.

Merton, R. 1973. "Theory of Rational Option Pricing." *Bell Journal of Economics and Management Science* 4 (1): 141–83.

Metz, C. 2017. "Google's AlphaGo Trounces Humans—but It Also Gives Them a Boost." *Wired*, May 26.

Miotto, R., L. Li, B. Kidd, and J. Dudley. 2016. "Deep Patient: An Unsupervised Representation to Predict the Future of Patients from Electronic Health Records." *Nature: Scientific Reports* 6: 26094.

Monk, A., D. Nadler, and D. Rook. 2016. "Startups Could Change the Way Big Investors Operate." *Harvard Business Review*, October 24.

———. 2017. "Data Management in Institutional Investing: A New Budgetary Approach." *SSRN* preprint, https://papers.ssrn.com/sol3/papers.cfm?abstract_id=3014911.

Monk, A., M. Prins, and D. Rook. 2019. "Rethinking Alternative Data in Institutional Investment." *Journal of Financial Data Science* (Winter).

Monk, A., and D. Rook. 2018. "Untangling Complexity for Comparative Advantage." *Centred Investor*, no. 10.

Monk, A., and R. Sharma. 2016. "'Organic Finance': The Incentives in Our Investment Products." *SSRN* preprint, https://papers.ssrn.com/sol3/papers.cfm?abstract_id= 2696448.

Mossin, J. 1966. "Equilibrium in a Capital Market Asset." *Econometrica* 34 (4): 768–83.

Nakamoto, S. 2008. "Bitcoin: A Peer-to-Peer Electronic Cash System." https://bitcoin .org/bitcoin.pdf.

Page, S. 2007. *The Difference: How the Power of Diversity Creates Better Groups, Firms, Schools, and Societies.* Princeton, NJ: Princeton University Press.

———. 2010. *Diversity and Complexity.* Princeton, NJ: Princeton University Press.

Petram, L., and L. Richards. 2014. *The World's First Stock Exchange.* New York: Columbia Business School.

Reed, S., and N. de Freitas. 2015. "Neural Programmer-Interpreters." https://arxiv.org/ abs/1511.06279.

Riley, J. 2017. "Understanding Metadata: What is Metadata, and What is it For?: A Primer." *NISO*. https://www.niso.org/publications/understanding-metadata-2017.

Rook, D., and A. Monk. 2018a. "Deep Geography: Implications of the Socio-spatial Structure in Artificial-Intelligence Research for Financial Institutions." https:// papers.ssrn.com/sol3/papers.cfm?abstract_id=3258050.

———. 2018b. "Managing Knowledge Management: Towards an Operating System for Institutional Investment." https://papers.ssrn.com/sol3/papers.cfm?abstract_id =3277989.

Savage, L. 1954. *The Foundations of Statistics.* New York: John Wiley and Sons.

Schelter, S., J-H. Bose, J. Kirschnick, T. Klein, and S. Seufert. 2017. "Automatically Tracking Metadata and Provenance of Machine Learning Experiments." *Workshop on ML Systems*, NIPS 2017, http://learningsys.org/nips17/assets/papers/paper _13.pdf.

Sharpe, W. 1964. "Capital Asset Prices: A Theory of Market Equilibrium under Conditions of Risk." *Journal of Finance* 19 (3): 425–42.

———. 1966. "Mutual Fund Performance." *Journal of Business* 39 (1): 119–38.

Sheikh, A., and H. Qiao. 2009. "Non-normality of Market Returns: A Framework for Asset Allocation Decision-Making." *J.P. Morgan Asset Management.* https://am .jpmorgan.com/blobcontent/1383169198442/83456/11_438.pdf.

Silver, D., A. Huang, C. Maddison, A. Guez, L. Sifre, G. van den Driessche, J. Schrittwieser, et al. 2016. "Mastering the Game of Go with Deep Neural Networks and Tree Search." *Nature* (529): 484–89.

Silver, D., J. Schrittwieser, K. Simonyan, I. Antonoglou, A. Huang, A. Guez, T. Hubert, et al. 2017. "Mastering the Game of Go without Human Knowledge." *Nature* (550): 354–59.

Smit, H., and L. Trigeorgis. 2004. *Strategic Investment: Real Options and Games.* Princeton, NJ: Princeton University Press.

Sornette, D. 2003. *Why Stock Markets Crash: Critical Events in Complex Financial Systems.* Princeton, NJ: Princeton University Press.

Taleb, N. 2007. *The Black Swan: The Impact of the Highly Improbable.* New York: Random House.

———. 2010. *The Bed of Procrustes: Philosophical and Practical Aphorisms.* New York: Penguin.

———. 2012. *Antifragile: How to Live in a World We Don't Understand.* London: Allen Lane.

———. 2018. *Skin in the Game: Hidden Asymmetries in Daily Life.* New York: Random House.

Tversky, A. 2004. *Preference, Belief, and Similarity: Selected Writings.* Cambridge, MA: MIT Press.

Voosen, P. 2017. "How AI Detectives Are Cracking Open the Black Box of Deep Learning." *Science,* July 6.

Wust, K., and A. Gervais. 2017. "Do You Need a Blockchain?" *Cryptology ePrint Archive,* https://eprint.iacr.org/2017/375.pdf.

Zoph, B., V. Vasudevan, J. Shlens, and Q. Le. 2017. "Learning Transferable Architectures for Scalable Image Recognition." https://arxiv.org/abs/1707.07012.

INDEX

of external, 153–54; underprioritizing of, 32. *See also* portable lessons
"innovation destiny," 154
innovation frameworks, 150–51
innovation teams, 155–57, 168, 170–72, 174
Inpher, 47, 143, 193n15
institutional-investment organization model, 63, 66
Intelligent Investor, The (Graham), 7, 190n8
intent in searches, 98
interconvertibility of data, information, knowledge, 9
interim monetization, 139
internally facing search engines, 135
internal operations, 59–60, 92, 151
internet, 21, 38, 202n14
interpersonal exchange, 20, 65, 73
interpretability of algorithms, 185
interviewing experts, 41, 80, 156, 179
intrinsic value, 57, 134
investable assets, 51, 115, 134–35, 141
investment portfolio, 3, 72, 115, 151, 164
investor-relevance, 170
Investors as long-term asset owners, 2, 36, 165
invest-tech, 18, 22; "breakthrough," 17; history of, 16–22; inferential depth and data latency, 38, 51; local and isolated, 34; technologized Investors and, 74–75; three-dimensional framework, 51
iOS operating systems, 39
isolated perspectives, 34–35
iterative: exchanges, 46; experimentation, 149; paradigm, 178

JavaScript, 99
JIRA, 47

joint ventures, 142–43
Jupyter Notebooks, 47, 86, 197n9

kaizen, 159–60, 201n12
Kensho search engine, 124
KKs (known knowns), 60–61
KM (knowledge management), 122–25
Knightian uncertainty, 114
knowledge: convertible into information, 114, 123; as data, 78; as distilled, aggregated information, 85; graphing, 124; and KM (knowledge management), 55, 85, 122–25; knowable and unknowable, 60–61; location of, 123–24; as power, 78; in resource hierarchy, 56; unknown versus unknowable, 194n11
KPIs (key performance indicators), 152–53
KUs (known unknowns), 60–61

large-scale projects, 30–31, 39, 70, 103, 156–57
latency, data, 17–23, 38, 51, 190n4, 191n7 (ch1), 192n2
launchpads, 180
leadership, 72, 148, 168–70, 173
leapfrogging, 5–8
learning culture, 2 (ch10), 147–49, 161–63, 200nn1, 202n14
legacy technology, 6, 39–40, 107, 144
lessons: "Lessons Learned" database, NASA's, 125. *See also* best practices; portable lessons
linked data fields, 191n11
LinkedIn, 122, 124
liquidity dashboard, 105–6
long-term asset owners, 2, 36, 165
long-term risk management, 116–17, 120, 126, 185

security of cloud-based storage, 107–8

seeding budgets, 157–58

selectivity, 111, 117, 128–31, 139–40, 150, 200n1 (ch9)

self-critical investors, 69, 73–74

self-help for users, 88

self-service needs, 87

semantic search, 98

separability of assets, 139

shadow-tracking algorithms, 121

Sharpe ratio, 115

short-termism, 3, 31, 44, 189n4

silos and fragmentation, 28–30, 69–70

simplicity, 38, 114–15, 131

skepticism, data, 196n10

skill profiles, 172–73, 178

skill versus luck, 122, 126, 137

skunkworks, 202n4

Slack, 47, 124, 193n14

smart assistants, 48

smart contracts, 126, 140–42, 187

smart diversification, 111

smart execution, 125–26

social-media data, 44–45

soft side of data and empowerment, 86–88

Sources of Advantage, 64, 68–69, 194n1

sourcing innovation, 153–55

S&P 500, 102, 137

"space to innovate," 68, 73, 144–46, 157, 160–61

spatial separation, 69

speed-depth tradeoff, 21, 190n5

spreadsheets: ancient examples of, 18; audit results on, 191n10; and biased thinking, 24; dark data in, 196n6; macro functionality in, 102; moving beyond, 95, 104–6, 164, 191n11;

performance issues of, 23–24; tyranny of, addiction to, 22–23

staging areas, 109

standardization of data, 19, 83–86, 196n6

Stanford University, 39, 146–47

statistical artifacts, 134

stock market, 7, 43–44

stock-ticker machines, 20

storage and access architectures. *See* databases

Stox, 48

strengths-centered innovation, 171

structural metadata, 97

studied learning, 149

substitutions and synergies, 54–55

success, defining, 168–71

suitability of technology, 17, 34, 50–51, 53, 65

superheroes: Clark Kent versus Bruce Wayne, 167; designing, 63; and sidekicks, 165; Superman, 121; technologizing by, 1; and traps, 3, 127–31, 141

superpower(s), 77; assessing, 50–51; building of, 1, 3–4, 168; cooperativity as, 141–43; culture and, 66, 148; data empowerment as, 67, 78–80; knowledge as, 37; learning culture as, 148; limitations to, 49; search functionality as, 49; self-improving, 26; technological, 68–69, 177

synergies and substitutions, 50–51, 54–55

Tableau, 106

tags, 98. *See also* metadata tools

talent as "built, bought, or borrowed," 160–61

TaskRabbit, 199n21

TDH (The Disruption House), 135, 153